The Love Language That Matters Most

THE LOVE LANGUAGE™ THAT MATTERS MOST

How to Personalize Love So They Really Feel It

Gary Chapman and
Les & Leslie Parrott

#1 NEW YORK TIMES BESTSELLING AUTHORS

NORTHFIELD PUBLISHING
CHICAGO

Edited by Connor Sterchi
Interior design: Puckett Smartt
Cover design: Faceout Studios, Kaylee Lockenour Dunn

ISBN: 978-0-8024-3890-4

We hope you enjoy this book from Northfield Publishing. Our goal is to provide high-quality, thought-provoking books and products that connect truth to your real needs and challenges. For more information on other books and products that will help you with all your important relationships, go to northfieldpublishing .com or write to:

Northfield Publishing
820 N. LaSalle Boulevard
Chicago, IL 60610

1 3 5 7 9 10 8 6 4 2

Printed in the United States of America

Contents

INTRODUCTION

Why Love Is a Language Worth Mastering

Whenever I'm speaking to a group or doing an interview about *The 5 Love Languages*, someone almost invariably asks, "Which of the five is most important?" It's a great question, and my answer is always the same: *The most important love language is the one that matters most to the person in front of you—your loved one.*

You see, love isn't about what feels natural to us, it's about what speaks directly to the heart of the other person. If you've read *The 5 Love Languages*, you know that we all have a primary love language, and when someone learns to express love in our language, it resonates deeply—it fills our emotional tank.

The challenge, of course, is learning another's love language and speaking it with fluency. Too many think that simply identifying another's love language means they'll automatically start speaking it. Not so.

Let me say it clearly: Knowing your partner's love language doesn't mean you automatically speak it with fluency. Far from it. Like any skill, a foreign love language takes practice, intentionality, and mastery. Knowing your partner's love language is only the first step—the real transformation happens when you learn how to consistently express love in their personalized vernacular. That's when you're speaking the love language that matters most.

And that's what this book is all about—moving beyond the basics and taking a deep dive into the dialects and nuances of your loved one's love language. You can think of *The 5 Love Languages* as the foundational course and *The Love Language That Matters Most* as your masterclass. These two books go together. They're companions.

My Coauthors

This brings me to my friends and coauthors, Les and Leslie Parrott. I've known this husband-wife team for more than thirty years. We met not long after *The 5 Love Languages* was first published in 1992. They were fresh out of their doctoral programs—Les, a new psychologist and Leslie a new marriage and family therapist. Every so often we found ourselves on the same talk shows or speaking platforms. So I've long respected their work.

In fact, when it came time to create the **5 Love Languages Premium Assessment**, I leaned on Les and Leslie to help me create it. If you're not familiar with the Premium Assessment, it's a powerful online tool that generates a beautiful fifteen-page report that not only identifies and clarifies your love language but also uncovers the unique nuances that make your expressions of love truly personal. It goes beyond the basics, helping you discover the specific ways you and your partner feel most loved.

5LoveLanguages.com/Premium

Les and Leslie are specialists in helping couples grow closer by learning to "translate" their love in the most impactful ways. Our goal together in this book isn't perfection—it's progress. It's about moving closer to your partner's heart, one intentional act at a time. Because when you take the time to love someone in the specific dialect of their love language, day after day, you're not just expressing affection—you're saying, "I see you, I value you, and I'm willing to meet you where you are." That's the kind of love that transforms relationships. And it's the love language that matters most.

Les, Leslie, and I are also partnering together to build out an entire network of trained and certified 5 Love Languages Coaches to help leverage your understanding and practice of the love languages in your personal relationships. You can see the special section at the back of this book if you're interested in learning more.

Mastering the Love Language That Matters Most

Learning to love at the most meaningful level is daring. It requires courage and commitment. Why? Because we're sure to stumble. After all, exploring the workings of another's heart is complex. You're bound to miss the mark.

So remember: It's not about perfection, it's about progress. It happens every time you brave the potential for fumbling and stumbling and do your best to speak the language of love yet again.

That's progress.

Still, you might be wondering when you've actually mastered your partner's love language. We'll tell you: You know you're becoming a master every time your partner feels seen, valued, and cherished. Their eyes light up, their demeanor softens, and your connection deepens.

But there's another important indicator: You know you're becoming a master whenever your loving efforts become second nature and feel intuitive—when you're no longer "trying" but you're naturally expressing love in ways that resonate deeply with your loved one because you know their dialect as if it were your own. That's when you're speaking their love language with fluency. That's when you're speaking the love language that matters most. And that's what we're going to show you in the pages of this book.

PART ONE

THE PROBLEM

The barriers to love
often hide in plain sight,
as we navigate
misunderstood gestures,
unmet needs, and the challenge
of speaking a language
that isn't our own.

CHAPTER 1

Lost in Translation

It was a moment of clarity I'll never forget—what says "I love you" to one person might not mean a thing to another.

How did it happen? A couple walked into my office for their first counseling session. I later learned they had been married for thirty years. The wife spoke first—without hesitation:

"Let me tell you a little bit about us before we start," she began. "We don't argue. We don't believe in arguing. We don't have money problems." She rattled off a few more positives, then her tone shifted. "But the problem is . . . I don't feel any love from him. We're like roommates. He does his thing, I do mine, and nothing is happening between us. I feel so empty inside. And honestly? I don't know how much longer I can go on like this."

I turned to her husband. He sighed, shaking his head. "I don't understand her. I do everything I can to show her that I love her. But she keeps saying she doesn't feel it. I don't know what else I can do."

So I asked, "What do you do to show her you love her?"

He didn't hesitate. "I get home before she does, so I start dinner. Sometimes I have it ready when she gets home. If not, we cook together. I wash the dishes. I vacuum the floors every Thursday night. I walk the dog every day. On Saturdays, I wash the car, mow the lawn, help with the laundry," he continued, listing off even more ways he cared for her. Then he looked at me, exasperated. "I don't know what else I can do."

I turned back to his wife. She nodded. "He's right. He works hard. But we don't talk. We haven't had a real conversation in twenty years. He's always doing things—washing dishes, mowing the grass, fixing the car—but he never just sits down and talks with me."

And in that moment, I saw it so clearly. Here was a man who deeply loved his wife, yet she didn't feel it. He was expressing love in a way that made sense to him. And while she appreciated all he did, it wasn't meeting her emotional need for love. What she longed for was meaningful conversation.

That experience was just the beginning. Over and over, I heard the same story—different details, same disconnect. I knew there had to be a pattern, but I couldn't quite put my finger on it. So I did something most people don't do—I went back and studied my own counseling notes—years' worth of them. I asked myself, "When someone said, 'I don't feel loved,' what were they really asking for?"

The answers fell into five clear patterns—what I later named the five love languages. And when couples started speaking the right one, everything changed. Walls came down. Connections deepened. Love finally landed.

Five years later, I had a thought: *If I could put this concept in a book, in everyday language, without the psychological jargon, maybe I could help people beyond the walls of my office—people I would never have the chance to counsel in person.*

I never imagined how far that book would go. Over the years, couples have told me it saved their marriage. Parents have said it changed the way they love their children. Friends, coworkers, even entire communities have applied these principles to strengthen their relationships.

Why? Because one of our deepest emotional needs is to feel loved by the people who matter most to us. If you're married, that person is your spouse. When you feel loved by your spouse, life is beautiful. But when you don't, even the best parts of life can feel empty.

Consider a couple of examples that may sound familiar . . .

Elliot stood at the stove, a trail of flour dusting his shirt. Dirty pots and pans filled the sink. The kitchen smelled of vanilla, sugar, and hope. He glanced at the timer—ten minutes until the soufflé would emerge, the pièce de résistance of the dinner he'd spent hours preparing.

He wanted to show Claire, who was working late at the office, how much he cared, how much he noticed her stress, her exhaustion. Knowing that acts of service is her love language, Elliot was confident in his grand gesture. He set the table and lit two candles. He couldn't wait to see Claire's eyes light up.

When Claire walked in, her heels clicking across the tile floor, Elliot turned to her with a proud smile. "Surprise!" he said, sweeping a hand toward the table. She paused in the doorway, her coat still on. "What's all this?" she asked with a puzzled face.

"It's dinner. I thought you might like a break after your long workday," Elliot said, his excitement faltering. Claire set her bag down, still trying to read the unexpected situation.

"Elliot, this is . . . really sweet. Really. But I already ate at the office. They ordered pizza for the late meeting," she said, rubbing her temples. "And honestly, if you don't mind, babe, I'm so tired—I'd love to take a hot shower and fall into bed."

"Oh," he said quietly while staring at the soufflé rising perfectly in the oven while his heart sank. He was doing his best to mask his disappointment and frustration.

Claire looked at him and sighed, softer this time. "Honey, you are so darling. I didn't mean to hurt your feelings," she said, walking toward him. "This really is thoughtful. I love you so much. I'm just . . . I'm just so exhausted."

Forcing a smile, Elliot nodded and blew out the candles.

He'd worked so hard to speak Claire's love language, to offer what he thought she wanted. He was on target with her love language but wasn't speaking quite right. Claire craved acts of service, for sure, but she craved the kind of service that was more practical. For her, coming home to a spotless kitchen or folded laundry was more likely to fill her love tank than a soufflé. Elliot's dinner, despite the good intentions, felt like pressure to Claire, not relief.

Elliot's love for Claire got lost in translation.

Maya knows the feeling. She was sitting cross-legged on the living room floor, nervously tapping her pen against her notebook. She knew words of affirmation was Matt's love language. It was something they'd talked about while reading *The 5 Love Languages*. She wanted to be intentional, to make him feel supported for a speech he was giving at a retirement event for his father—something that made him very self-conscious. Encouragement didn't come naturally to Maya, so she rehearsed what she wanted to say to Matt, determined to get it right.

When Matt came in from mowing the lawn, Maya greeted him with a bright smile. "Hey, you're going to crush it tomorrow," she said confidently. "You've worked so hard, and I just know everyone's going to be blown away."

Matt smiled, but it didn't reach his eyes. "Thanks," he said. He gave her a quick kiss on the cheek before heading to his home office for some final prep.

That wasn't the reaction Maya expected. Maybe he needed to hear it again. "Seriously, Matt," she said, leaning against the doorframe. "You're going to nail it. You've been preparing for two weeks, and there's no way it'll go wrong. You're the best person to honor your dad."

Matt managed a strained smile. "Thanks, Maya. I appreciate it."

Maya knew her words weren't landing. So later that evening, as they got ready for bed she asked: "Is something wrong? I've been trying to encourage you, but it feels like I'm not helping."

Matt sighed, rubbing the back of his neck. "It's not that I don't appreciate what you're saying," he said carefully. "It's just . . . the way you're saying it. When you tell me how great I'm going to do, it feels like . . . like I don't know, like I can't mess up. Like if I don't nail this, I'll be letting my dad down—or you."

Maya's heart sank. "That's not what I meant at all," she said quickly. "I just wanted you to feel confident because I love you."

"I know," Matt said gently, "but I think what I need isn't confidence right now. It's . . . reassurance. I need to know that no matter how tomorrow goes, you're proud of me and love me just the same. That it's okay if I'm not perfect."

Maya teared up. She realized that her words added to the pressure he was already carrying. He didn't need a pep talk, he needed to know that he was enough, no matter the outcome.

Like Elliot, she knew her partner's love language, but as much as she wanted to speak it, something was still getting lost in translation.

That (Not So) Loving Feeling

It's a disheartening experience—pouring your energy into showing love, believing you've cracked the code, only to watch it land with a dull thud. You replay the moment in your mind, searching for where it went wrong. Maybe it was the timing. Maybe it was the delivery. Maybe it was you.

Your intention was good, your heart was in the right place, and yet, the response wasn't what you hoped for. It's not only disappointing—it's deflating. You feel unseen in your attempt to make your loved one feel seen.

And then comes the doubt. You wonder if you'll ever get it right, if the gap between what you give and what they crave is just too wide to bridge. Frustration creeps in. Why didn't this work? What am I missing? The vulnerability of trying to express your love, only to miss the mark, can make you want to stop trying altogether. But mixed in with the frustration is a lingering ache, because all you wanted was to make them feel loved. And instead, you're left with the nagging sense that you've failed—not in loving them, but in speaking their love language in the way they long to hear it.

These moments are raw. They remind us how challenging love can be, even with the best intentions. But if you've ever felt this ache, you're not alone. Misfires in love are part of the love language journey.

Why Loving Intentions Can Get Lost in Translation

When we get an answer to *why*, it paves the path for *how*. Knowing *why* our attempts to love aren't working transforms our confusion into clarity, frustration into purpose. Research shows that understanding the reason behind a struggle keeps us from spinning in circles or doubling down on strategies that aren't connecting.[1] The answer to *why* provides insight that allows us to pivot, refine, and ultimately succeed.

Because this book is devoted to the *how*—how to speak any of the five love languages with fluency—it's worth pausing to consider the *why* first. Why do our loving expressions sometimes fall short? Here are half a dozen of the most common reasons.

Speaking the Right Language for the Wrong Reason

Let's get this one cleared up right from the start. Sometimes, attempts to speak a partner's love language come from an insincere place. When the motivation is to influence a partner's actions or emotions—like giving words of affirmation to elicit praise in return or performing acts of service to gain leverage in an argument—the gesture loses its authenticity. Love isn't something you can check off your to-do list. Even if the language is technically correct, the lack of sincerity is bound to come through, leaving the other person feeling uneasy, used, or suspicious. Love languages only work when the intention is to connect, not control. And it's not a task to accomplish. It's a matter of the heart.

Attempts to manipulate love languages erode the trust that allows genuine connection to flourish. Research from social psychologists supports this: People are remarkably adept at detecting insincerity, even if it's subtle.[2] When a partner senses that a loving gesture is "giving in order to get," it triggers feelings of resentment rather than intimacy. Love, at its core, is a language that only "works" when the goal is to give, not gain. Later in this book, we'll explore practical ways to avoid falling into the trap of turning love into a calculated exchange.

Neglecting a Secondary Love Language

The 5 Love Languages explains how everyone has a primary love language, one that resonates most deeply. But it's rarely the only way that person feels loved. A secondary love language can be incredibly important and neglecting it can lead to feelings of disconnection or dissatisfaction. For instance, someone whose primary love language is physical touch might also need words of affirmation to feel truly loved and valued. If their partner focuses exclusively on holding hands, hugs, and cuddles without offering verbal encouragement or appreciation, it may leave a gap that physical touch alone can't fill.

Without some versatility in your partner's secondary love language, your expression of love may be incomplete. A partner may wonder, *Why don't I feel as fulfilled as I should when they're trying so hard?* This disconnect can be especially evident when you're putting in the effort, but your partner isn't feeling it. We know this reality requires you to be "multilingual" in love. Don't worry, we're going to show you how to do that in a later chapter.

The "Fluent in All Five" Phenomenon

Every so often we hear from someone who says, "My wife says she needs all of the love languages." They light up at kind words, cherish thoughtful gifts, melt with physical touch, relish quality time, and appreciate every act of service. They claim they don't have a primary love language, insisting they want "all of them." While this versatility might seem like a relationship bonus, it can actually create a unique challenge: Their partner may struggle to know where to focus. It can be overwhelming, leaving their partner feeling uncertain or inadequate, unsure if their efforts are truly making an impact. This can lead to frustration or exhaustion as they try to meet what feels like an endless demand for affection.

So what's behind this statement? In all likelihood, this person *does* have one or two love languages that resonate most deeply. The reason they "want all of them" is due to a *love deficit*. They may be so eager for love that they want it in *all* its expressions. Their love tank is perpetually low so they'll take any and every drop of love they can get to feel valued and cherished. This longing for love in every language often points to unmet needs or past emotional neglect, leaving them unsure of what truly fills their tank (more on this later). We recommend taking the 5 Love Languages Premium Assessment. It's the quickest way to get to the bottom of which love language rises to the top. It will give both partners clarity and direction for more meaningful connections.

The Dialect Disconnect

Head to Houston and you'll hear a blend of Southern and Western influences in their dialect, with distinct pronunciations like "fixin' to" and "y'all." Boston is famous for dropping the "r" sound ("pahk the cah"). In Philadelphia you'll hear vowel shifts, like "wooder" for water. The dialect in Chicago features flat "a" sounds ("maaan" for man). The Deep South is known for its melodic intonation and elongated vowels, as well as phrases like "bless your heart."

They're all speaking the same language: English. But the dialects are often dramatically different. And every love language has a variety of languages within it. Each love language is universal in concept, but deeply personal in practice. Each person has a unique "dialect" within their primary love language—a specific and personalized way they interpret and receive love.

Remember Elliot and Claire from our introduction? Elliot was spot-on in knowing that Claire's primary love language is acts of service. But he was missing her dialect. She loves acts of service that save her time and give her more margin. But he was going for grand gestures, like making her a soufflé.

When we focus only on the broad strokes of a love language and miss its nuances, our gestures can feel generic rather than personal, leaving our partner's love tank only partially filled. Not only that, we feel disheartened, thinking, *I'm trying so hard—why isn't this working?* To truly connect, we've got to go beyond the broad category of someone's love language and learn the subtleties of their dialect.

That's why the third part of this book ("The Tactics") is devoted entirely to uncovering and understanding your partner's dialects. In the five chapters of Part Three, you'll find practical steps and strategies to go beyond the basics of love languages and discover the unique expressions that will mean the most to your partner.

Personality Differences

You can't separate love languages from personality. That's like trying to separate flavor from food or melody from music. Personality types are baked into the DNA of our being, influencing every expression of love. They come part and parcel with whatever love language we're attempting to speak.

Two people with the same primary love language may still interpret and experience it very differently depending on their personality. For instance, an extrovert who thrives on social energy might feel loved when words of affirmation are given publicly, like in front of friends or family, while an introvert might find the same gesture uncomfortable, preferring private, heartfelt conversations. When personality isn't factored in, even well-meaning efforts can feel misaligned, leaving one partner feeling unseen and the other confused about why their efforts aren't landing.

Understanding personality differences helps us navigate these dynamics, allowing us to speak our partner's love language in ways that are meaningful and natural for them. We've devoted an entire upcoming chapter to personality and its impact on love languages. It's a key factor in fostering emotional closeness. When we integrate personality into how we express love, we significantly improve how fluent we become in speaking another's love language.

Mistaking Sympathy for Empathy

One of the most common reasons our love languages can get lost in translation is found in a lack of empathy—that capacity we all have to put ourselves in another's shoes and see the world from their perspective. I've heard Les and Leslie say it countless times from the stage: "The happiest couples on the planet are those who enjoy mutual empathy." It's difficult to exaggerate the importance empathy plays in helping you to become fluent in speaking the love language your partner longs to hear.

We often confuse empathy with sympathy. Both involve care and concern, but they come from fundamentally different places. Sympathy focuses on feeling *for* someone—acknowledging their pain or struggle. It's more of an observation from a distance. Empathy, on the other hand, is about feeling *with* someone—stepping into their world and experiencing their emotions alongside them. It's a game changer.

When we offer empathy instead of sympathy, we bridge the emotional gap and create a connection that goes beyond surface-level concern. Empathy says, "I see you, I hear you, and I'm here with you," while sympathy can unintentionally stop at: "I feel bad for you." Sympathy, while well-meaning, can even feel patronizing. But don't worry, we've got you covered. Les and Leslie are leading experts in empathy. They've devoted years to studying and teaching the art of empathy in relationships, and you'll discover their sometimes counterintuitive wisdom in upcoming chapters.

The Path to Fluency

So there you have it. Six of the most common reasons our expressions of love can get lost in translation—whether it's struggling to uncover a partner's unique dialect, overlooking personality differences, or mistaking sympathy for empathy. Each of these challenges is real, but none are insurmountable. All it takes is a willing heart and motivation.

When famed chef Julia Child first moved to France, she didn't speak a word of French. Determined to immerse herself in the culture she loved, she enrolled in cooking school and began learning the language. At first, her accent was comical, and she frequently mixed up words, asking for "poison" instead of "poisson" (fish) at the market. But Julia's enthusiasm and persistence won people over. Eventually, she not only mastered French but used it to bring the joy of cooking to American kitchens, quirks and all.

In the chapters ahead, we'll guide you through your own journey of mastering the language of love. Just like Julia Child's determination transformed her from a novice to a beloved expert, your willingness to embrace the process is all that's required.

We start by exploring your partner's proverbial love tank. This simple metaphor of emotional reserves holds profound insights into why some relationships thrive while others get stuck. So get ready to learn how to recognize when the tank is running low, what it takes to fill it up, and how to keep it from running on fumes.

YOUR TURN

Based on what you learned in this chapter, which of the six reasons is most likely to cause your loving intentions to get lost in translation and why?

CHAPTER 2

Solving the Mystery of a Low Love Tank

Captain Martin Whittaker leaned forward in his seat, studying the blinking lights on the fuel gauges. Something wasn't right. At 35,000 feet, with the Boeing 747 cutting through the clouds on its way from London to sunny Spain, the readings on the instrument panel had gone from reassuring to confusing in a matter of moments.

"Do you see this?" he asked his first officer, his voice steady but with a sharpness that made his concern clear.

The first officer nodded, leaning closer to the display. "Could be a faulty sensor," he suggested, though the doubt in his tone mirrored Whittaker's.

The captain's jaw tightened as he considered the options. "Faulty" wasn't a word he liked to rely on mid-flight, especially when hundreds of passengers sat obliviously behind him, sipping their drinks and leafing through in-flight magazines. The Atlantic Ocean stretched beneath them—a vast, unyielding expanse.

Whittaker reached for the radio. "This is British Airways Flight 32. We're experiencing irregular fuel readings and request clearance to divert to Lisbon."

The response crackled through the headset, calm and clipped. "BA32, you're cleared for an emergency landing at Lisbon. Runway 27. Winds are calm. Proceed when ready."

The next twenty minutes were a masterclass in precision and focus. He adjusted course, calculated glide paths, and carefully rationed the remaining fuel. Every decision felt like walking a tightrope, balancing between hope and catastrophe.

As the plane began its descent, Whittaker finally allowed himself a glance at the fuel indicators. The needles were dangerously low, hovering just above empty. The aircraft touched down with the faintest shudder, rolling to a stop on the Lisbon runway. The silence in the cockpit was deafening.

It wasn't until they were safely on the ground that the truth emerged: a clerical error had nearly cost them everything. Ground staff back in London had refueled the plane using pounds instead of kilograms, giving the aircraft less than half the fuel it needed. The realization was maddening in its simplicity—an avoidable mistake that could have had tragic consequences.

Just as that British Airways flight was nearly grounded by a simple miscalculation, our relationships falter when we don't pay attention to what fuels them. Love tanks run dry not because we don't care, but because we assume they're fuller than they are. We too often misjudge their emotional refueling. This chapter is your guide to ensuring that doesn't happen, offering pragmatic tools for checking your emotional gauges and keeping your relationship aloft.

What Exactly Is a Love Tank?

Fred Rogers, affectionately known as Mister Rogers, once said: "I feel so strongly that deep and simple is far more essential than shallow and complex."[3] It's a timeless truth. And we think Fred would have appreciated the concept of an emotional love tank. It's profoundly simple and deeply impactful.

At its core, a love tank is a metaphor for the emotional reservoir inside each of us—a place where affection, care, and attention from others are stored. When our love tank is full, we feel valued, secure, and connected. We're energized to give love in return, and our relationships flourish. But when our tank runs low or even empties, we ache for closeness, feel the sting of being unseen, and become exhausted from our emotional reserves being siphoned.

Everyone has a love tank. It's part of what makes us human. From the moment we take our first breath, we thrive on love and connection. A baby's delighted coo at a parent's tender embrace is more than a heart-warming moment. It's evidence that the baby's love tank is being filled. As children, we're deeply attuned to this emotional reservoir, instinctively responding to how much affection and attention we're receiving. When it's full, we flourish, and when it's empty, we disconnect.

This intrinsic need for love doesn't fade as we grow older. If anything, it becomes more apparent as adults. While we might learn to mask the signs of an empty tank, the impact remains the same: growing frustration, emotional disconnection, and a lingering sense of being unloved. As it fills, however, we feel more and more secure, connected, and energized in our relationship.

What You May Not Know About a Love Tank

At first glance, the concept of a love tank might seem straightforward—keep it full, and your relationship will thrive. That's true. But there's more to it than meets the eye. What seems simple is often more of a mystery—why someone's tank stays low even when love is being expressed can defy logic. Understanding the workings of a love tank means recognizing four key truths: It needs the right fuel, it changes quickly, it drains faster than it fills, and it comes in different sizes. Let's unpack each of these.

It Needs the Right Fuel

Everyone knows that a car's engine relies on the right fuel to run. Some require high octane, some diesel, some ethanol, and some electricity. The type of fuel isn't a matter of preference—it's essential to the engine's performance. A love tank works the same way. To be fueled properly, it requires the expressions of love that resonate most deeply with that person.

The 5 Love Languages emphasizes the importance of knowing your partner's love language. You know that when you give the wrong kind of love, it's like putting diesel into a gas engine: Your efforts won't fill their love tank. But as you make your way through *The Love Language That Matters Most*, you'll become more adept at speaking their love language with fluency. And it's that fluency, with all its dialectical nuance, that fuels their love tank faster, easier, consistently, and with more enduring impact. It all comes down to really knowing your partner's "fuel type."

It Changes Quickly

A love tank is rarely static. As folks down south like to say, it can change faster than melting butter on a hot biscuit. The level of a love tank fluctuates. It aligns with what your loved one needs in any particular moment.

For instance, if your partner is feeling overwhelmed, an act of service—like helping with a chore—might fill their love tank more quickly than at other times. Why? Because it's not just the action—it's the timing. By recognizing and responding to their immediate experience, their love language cuts through the noise and fills up their tank more quickly than it might during moments when their needs aren't as pressing or clear.

The dynamic nature of a love tank requires attentiveness and flexibility. It's not always enough to rely on what worked earlier. Thriving relationships are built on continually tuning in to your partner's emotional state and loving them in the way they need it most in that moment.

By the way, you might be wondering: Is it realistic to keep your partner's love tank full every single day? The honest answer is no. Life is full of ups and downs, and expecting that kind of consistency is more than unrealistic—it's impossible. Relationships are built on progress, not perfection. Grace, not guilt. What matters most is the intentional effort to notice and refill the tank when it's running low.

It Drains Faster than It Fills

Chapter 2 of *The 5 Love Languages* goes in depth about the consequences of a low love tank and how we can keep a love tank full. One of the most surprising aspects of a love tank is how quickly it can be drained. Small, unintentional missteps—like a harsh tone, unmet expectations, or distractions—can deplete your partner's reserves faster than you might realize.

Renowned researcher John Gottman, at the University of Washington, found that it takes at least five positive interactions to counterbalance the impact of one negative interaction in a relationship. This is often referred to as the "Magic Ratio," and it highlights just how much emotional weight even a small moment of negativity can carry. A single dismissive comment or forgotten gesture can siphon love from the tank far faster than a kind word or act can replenish it.

So if you're serious about filling up your partner's love tank, you need to be as intentional about what causes it to leak as you are with what fills it up. In other words, you've got to be mindful of "love leaks." They aren't always obvious—they can be the result of unspoken frustrations or unfounded perceptions.

The key is awareness. When you actively pay attention to your partner's needs and emotional state, you can catch these leaks before they drain too much. Mindfulness, paired with intentional acts of love—that counterbalance the negative—creates a balance that keeps your partner's tank fuller, longer.

It Comes in Different Sizes

Not all love tanks are created equal. Some people have large emotional reservoirs, while others have smaller, more sensitive tanks. Those with larger tanks may not require as much attention to keep them full. On the other hand, someone with a smaller tank might feel the impact of even small gestures—both positive and negative—much more acutely.

This difference in "tank size" isn't about one being better or worse. It's simply a reflection of past experiences and emotional needs. A person who grew up in a nurturing home with steady emotional reinforcement is likely to have a larger tank that feels naturally fuller, more robust. Conversely, someone who experienced inconsistency or neglect in their formative years might have a smaller tank, requiring more frequent attention to stay filled.

Here's a quick comparison:

	Small Love Tank	Large Love Tank
Early Life	Experienced inconsistent expressions of love	Experienced consistent nurturing expressions of love
Capacity	Fills quickly but empties just as fast	Takes longer to fill but retains contentment longer
Sensitivity	Small disturbances cause noticeable spillage	Small disturbances can often go unnoticed

Response to Love	Reacts strongly to even small loving gestures	Requires repeated gestures to get a noticeable response
Response to Neglect	Quickly shows signs of emptiness, such as irritability or withdrawal	Gradually shows signs of slow emotional disconnection
Maintenance	Requires frequent refilling	Takes more effort to fill over time

So how do you know if your partner's love tank is big or small? Well, it begins by recognizing that tank size is measured in relationship to your own. If you have a naturally large emotional tank, meaning that you hold reserves of love pretty well, you might assume your partner experiences the same robust feelings of love that you do. Don't make that assumption. If your partner's tank is smaller than yours, you may need to be more consistent in filling it up than what you require. Like we said, it's relative.

The bottom line is to be mindful of how sensitive your partner might be to needing their love tank replenished. Holding them to your standard, if their tank is different, can lead to misunderstandings. The key is to step outside your own experience, consider your partner's early years, observe how frequently their tank is diminished, and adjust your approach to meet their unique capacity—not yours.

How to Gauge Your Partner's Love Tank

People often ask us: "What's the best way to know how full—or empty—my partner's love tank is?" Here's our answer: Ask them. The direct approach is often the most effective. You can ask questions like, "Do you feel loved by me lately?" or "What could I do to help you feel more cared for?" It's that simple.

For a playful twist, consider a scale: "On a scale of 1 to 10, where's your love tank today?" This lighthearted approach keeps the tone inviting while still digging into what your partner might be feeling. Of course, if their tank is running low, ask what you can do to fill it up.

When's the best time to check in? Love tanks can fluctuate daily—or even hourly—based on stress, interactions, and life's demands. That means there's never really a bad time to ask. Whether it's during a quiet evening together or in the middle of a busy day, regular check-ins help you stay tuned in to your partner's emotional state.

The key to gauging their love tank is consistency. A weekly check-in is great, but making it a regular habit ensures their emotional needs remain a priority. When you truly listen, notice, and respond, you're not just learning about their love tank—you're actively helping to fill it.

One more thing. Sometimes a person will mask the signs of an empty tank. If your partner doesn't openly share their feelings, you'll need to go into "scout mode." Look for the subtle signs that their love tank might be running low. Being in scout mode means paying attention to what's beneath the surface. It's about noticing patterns, staying curious, and gently opening the door for conversation when the time feels right. A simple observation like, "You seem a little off today—how can I help?" can make all the difference in helping your partner feel seen and understood.

How to Drain a Love Tank

While filling your partner's love tank takes time and effort, draining it can happen in an instant—and often unintentionally. One of the fastest ways to deplete a love tank can be summed up in a single word: ***neglect***. When your partner feels invisible or overlooked, even in the smallest ways, it can send a message that they don't matter. Forgetting a meaningful date, brushing off their concerns, or being distracted during quality time might seem minor in the moment, but over time, these small lapses add up and erode emotional reserves.

Consider Susan, who said, "While we were in a serious conversation, his phone rang. He answered it and started talking to a friend. I felt totally rejected." Her love tank quickly emptied.

Another surefire way to drain a love tank is through ***criticism***. Fault-finding, harsh words, or even subtle sarcasm can chip away at your partner's sense of emotional safety. Relationships thrive on kindness—regardless of your partner's love language. Even well-meaning "constructive feedback" can drain a love tank if it isn't delivered with love and sensitivity.

Lack of follow-through is another major drain. Patrick said: "She told me she would take my shirts to the cleaners. I said, wonderful! When I came home that afternoon, the shirts were lying in the same chair where I left them. My love tank emptied very quickly. She said: 'I'm sorry, I forgot.' Which to me was a poor excuse." Promising to do something and not delivering—whether it's something big, like a shared goal, or small, like taking out the trash—can leave your partner feeling disrespected. Over time, unkept promises can lead to a sense of distrust, which drains the love tank even further.

Finally, ***emotional withdrawal*** is one of the most damaging ways to drain a love tank. When you shut down, avoid vulnerability, or withhold affection, it creates a chasm in the relationship. Your partner's love tank can't be filled if the flow of connection is blocked.

Neglect, criticism, lack of follow-through, and emotional withdrawal are among the most common culprits behind a leaky love tank. The good news? Simply recognizing these behaviors is a powerful first step. Awareness allows you to address these issues head-on, whether by avoiding them altogether or making intentional efforts to repair the damage. With mindfulness and care, you can begin to "leak-proof" your partner's tank and strengthen the foundation of your relationship.

The Ripple Effect of Love Tanks

Here's a little secret: Love tanks don't exist in isolation. In a relationship, they're deeply interconnected, often creating a ripple effect between partners. When one person's tank is full, it naturally overflows into the relationship, making it easier for them to express love, patience, and kindness. Conversely, when one tank is running low, it can create a sense of strain, frustration, or even resentment, which can then impact the other partner's tank.

This dynamic means that neglecting your own emotional needs—or those of your partner—can set off a cycle that's hard to break. For example, a partner with an empty tank may unintentionally withdraw, leading the other to feel distance. Over time, this back-and-forth creates a downward spiral where both tanks are routinely running on fumes.

But the reverse is also true. Small, intentional efforts to fill your partner's tank—regardless of their love language—create positive momentum. Even a single act of love can shift the dynamic, making your partner feel seen, valued, and cared for. In turn, they're more likely to express love back to you, creating a ripple effect of connection and intimacy. In this way, keeping both tanks full becomes a shared responsibility.

Think back to Captain Whittaker, guiding his airplane safely to the ground despite an almost empty tank. His success wasn't just about skill—it was about attentiveness, quick adjustments, and an unwavering commitment to addressing the problem before it became catastrophic. Relationships require the same kind of care. A love tank doesn't stay full on its own, and ignoring it guarantees relational turbulence.

But just like Captain Whittaker made the right adjustments, you can too. Love tanks may drain faster than they fill, but with steady effort and learning to speak the love language your partner longs to hear, you'll soon build the emotional reserves to sustain your relationship. And while no tank stays full all the time, the commitment to noticing and refilling it ensures your relationship remains strong.

YOUR TURN

What actionable insight did you gain from this chapter about your own love tank? And your partner's? How will it change what you do?

CHAPTER 3

The #1 Challenge for Becoming Multilingual in Love

Years ago, Princeton psychologists John Darley and Daniel Batson conducted a now-famous study that has become a staple in social psychology courses.[4]

Here's what happened: The researchers asked a group of seminary students to prepare a short, impromptu talk. One by one, the students were told to walk to a nearby building on campus to deliver their presentation.

But on their way to the building, each student encountered a man staged by the researchers. He was slumped over, head down, coughing and groaning—clearly in need of help.

The question was simple: Who would stop to help?

To add depth to the study, Darley and Batson introduced a few key variables. For instance, they varied the topic of the students' talks. Some were asked to reflect on their vocation in ministry, while others were given the parable of the Good Samaritan—a story centered on helping someone in need.

They also manipulated the students' sense of urgency. For some, the experimenter glanced at his watch and said, "Oh, you're late. They were expecting you a few minutes ago. You'd better hurry." For others, he casually remarked, "It'll be a few minutes before they're ready for you, but you might as well head over now."

Now, which of these seminary students do you think was most likely to stop and help the man in need?

If you're like most people, you'd guess that the students preparing to speak on the parable of the Good Samaritan—the ultimate lesson in compassion—would be the ones most likely to stop. It seems obvious, right?

But here's the twist: We're wrong.

The results of the study are as surprising as they are unsettling. The topic of the talk—whether it was about the Good Samaritan or something entirely unrelated—had virtually no impact on whether the students stopped to help.

What made the difference? The sense of urgency.

Students who believed they were late were far less likely to stop, even if they were on their way to discuss the parable of the Good Samaritan. In fact, some of them stepped over the groaning man in their rush to get to their talk.

The study revealed a simple but profound truth: our actions are often shaped more by our immediate focus—our agenda—than by our values or intentions. It's human nature. We become so preoccupied with our own tasks that we can fail to recognize what matters most in the moment. And that's the number one challenge to speaking the love language that matters most.

Everybody's Got an Agenda

We'd like to think of ourselves as generous, attentive, and loving—especially when it comes to the person we love the most. But if we're honest, most of us have an agenda running in the background of our relationship.

It might not be selfish or even conscious, but it's there. It can simply be the mental checklist of everything you need to get done: "Pick up groceries. Call Mom. Schedule a dentist appointment. Make dinner." Whatever the case, your focus isn't entirely on your partner—it's on navigating your own priorities.

Our agendas aren't selfish or sinister (at least we hope so). Life is busy, and we all have responsibilities. But when our agenda takes center stage, it becomes nearly impossible to focus on someone else's love language, let alone their unique dialect. We delude ourselves into thinking we're focused on them when it's our own agenda that's actually getting the love.

Any of these sound familiar?

- Your partner loves hearing **words of affirmation**, and you know they've been craving a little extra encouragement. So on your way out the door, you toss over your shoulder a quick "You're amazing!" Sure, it's nice, but does it really resonate? Maybe. Or maybe not.
- You know your partner wants **quality time**, but the idea of an in-depth conversation feels overwhelming after a stressful day. So you half-listen while surreptitiously doomscrolling on your phone. Quality time? Hardly.
- Your partner is all about **acts of service**, so you quickly load the dishwasher before they come home. But you're eager to get to your Xbox and you leave the sink still piled high with dirty pans, leaving them to finish the job. Act of service? You got close.
- Your partner lights up when **receiving gifts**, so you surprise them with a book you thought they'd love. Turns out they already have it and told you about it awhile back. Oops.
- Your partner thrives on **physical touch**, and you know a warm hug after a tough day means the world to them. But instead of lingering, you give them a distracted pat on the back before heading to your laptop. Physical touch? Nada.

But can you really be blamed? You're not Mother Teresa, and nobody's expecting you to be. The good news is that you don't have to live up to saintly perfection to become fluent in your partner's love language. We'll say it once more: fluency is about progress, not perfection.

Is Your Agenda Sabotaging Your Love Life?

The problem isn't having an agenda—it's letting it run the show. When you allow self-focus to routinely dominate your interactions, you can count on your partner's love tank running low. Why? Because true connection requires more than just surface-level engagement. It requires an agenda-less presence.

Presence is more than being in the same room—it's about offering your undivided attention. It begins the moment when you put down your phone, silence your internal to-do list, and focus entirely on your partner. Presence says, *You matter to me, and I'm here for you.*

Presence and attention go hand in hand. This is critical to speaking the love language that matters most: Presence is about showing up emotionally and mentally, while attention ensures you're truly tuned in to your partner. Together, they say, *You're my priority in this moment.*

Without attention, presence becomes hollow—simply being there isn't enough. And without presence, attention lacks depth—listening to words without understanding their emotion falls short. It's in the union of both that love languages come alive, allowing you to notice the nuances of your partner's needs and respond in ways that feel personal and genuine.

So your own priorities and personal agenda may be important. But if they dominate your relationship, they're sabotaging your ability to love. They're canceling presence and attention. Love languages, by their very nature, ask you to step out of self-focus and into an other-focused mindset—a shift that requires intentionality and effort but yields profound connection.

Why We're Distracted by Default

If you've ever caught yourself nodding along to a conversation without really listening, or agreeing to something you didn't fully hear, welcome to being human. It happens. In fact, distraction is practically our human default.

Now more than ever, we live in a world designed to pull our attention in every direction. Notifications pinging, new updates, emails demanding a quick reply, schedules overflowing, and multitasking make it hard to focus on the person in front of us—even when they're the one we care about most. But it's not just modern life that gets in the way. It can be something beneath the surface.

Unmet Needs

You've probably heard of the acronym HALT. It stands for Hungry, Angry, Lonely, Tired. It's commonly used to remind people of the states that make them more vulnerable to poor decision-making or self-focused behavior. And it's no surprise: Any one of these elements can pull your attention inward and make it harder to focus on your partner.

Hunger triggers survival instincts, anger clouds your judgment, loneliness turns your thoughts toward unmet emotional needs, and fatigue saps the energy needed for meaningful connection. Research shows that when these needs aren't met, our brains prioritize coping over connecting. They amplify our self-focus. They become our primary agenda. The point? You can't speak anyone's language fluently when you're hungry, angry, lonely or tired. And neither can your partner.

Full Focus

It's not only unmet needs that pull us away from our partner—it can also be a deep focus on something that feels all-consuming. Whether it's a work deadline, a home improvement project, a ballgame you're watching, an entrepreneurial venture, or even writing a book (guilty as charged!), being immersed in a task can make it hard to pivot to your partner's needs.

Here's the tricky part: This kind of distraction often comes from good intentions or productive pursuits. You're working hard, making progress, or simply enjoying something you love. But even when your focus is positive, it can unintentionally leave your partner feeling overlooked or less important.

It's not that you mean to ignore them. It's that focus, by its very nature, has a limited supply. When we're fully locked in on one thing, everything else fades to the background—even the person who matters most. In these moments, we hope our partner can offer grace and patience. But beware: over time, these instances of hyperfocus can accumulate, leaving your partner feeling like they're competing with another passion—or worse, that they're not a priority at all.

Unseen Wounds

The third major distraction can hit hard for some: unresolved wounds. These might stem from childhood experiences, past relationships, or even lingering tensions within the current relationship. Counselors refer to this as "emotional residue"—feelings or fears carried over from past hurts that linger in our current interactions. Without realizing it, these wounds can shape how we respond to our partner's needs in ways that become automatic, even beyond our control.

Unresolved emotional wounds don't just fade with time. They resurface, often in unexpected ways. A fear of rejection might make you hesitant to open up emotionally. A history of feeling unworthy might lead you to downplay your partner's efforts to show love. Or perhaps past betrayals make it difficult for you to trust, even when your partner's intentions are pure.

These unseen wounds can act as filters through which we interpret our partner's words and actions. A simple request for more time together might feel like criticism. A moment of tension might trigger feelings of abandonment. Without awareness, these patterns can create distance, even in a relationship filled with good intentions and genuine care.

When emotional wounds go unaddressed, they don't just distract us from loving our partner—they keep us stuck. Stuck in self-protection. Stuck in fear. Stuck in a cycle where connection feels harder to sustain. And while our partner might sense something is off, they may not understand the deeper emotional weight we're carrying.

Owning our wounds is vital. As Franciscan priest Richard Rohr says, "You cannot heal what you do not first acknowledge."[5] So it's worth asking: *What unresolved hurts might be shaping the way I show up in my relationship?* Recognizing these patterns isn't easy, but it's vital to finding healing. After all, these wounds don't just distract us from loving our partner—they can also keep us from receiving their love. A trusted counselor or a Love Language Coach can help you process unresolved pain, untangle complex emotions, and develop tools for building healthier patterns of connection.

How to Get Over Yourself

If you've ever tried to speak another language, you know how tempting it is to translate everything back into your own tongue. It's natural to think in terms of what makes sense to *you*. But when it comes to love languages, this tendency creates a barrier that's hard to break.

The biggest obstacle to becoming fluent in love isn't just knowing the right words, giving the perfect gift, or checking the box on quality time—it's focusing too much on yourself, too often. Even with the best intentions, a self-focused mindset can quietly undermine your efforts. If you're going through the motions without truly prioritizing your partner, your attempts to speak their love language will fall flat. Guaranteed.

So how do you get over yourself? How do you temporarily set your personal agenda aside and fully focus on your partner? The answer isn't complicated, but it does require intention—and we've got a simple, proven plan to help you start.

Name Your Agenda

Name it to tame it. Ever heard that phrase? Psychiatrist Dr. Daniel Siegel came up with it to underscore the value of putting words to whatever's on our mind. It's a quick and easy way to find immediate emotional relief. It lowers anxiety and enables us to focus more intentionally on what we choose.

We recommend this method as a starting point for becoming more present and attentive. For example, before interacting with your partner, take a moment to ask yourself, *What's running through my mind right now?* Name whatever is preoccupying your thoughts. No need to say it out loud. It works just fine as internal dialogue. Maybe it's a looming deadline, or an errand that needs your attention. Naming your agenda helps you separate it from the interaction so you can consciously shift your focus and become less self-consumed.

Press Pause on Your Agenda

It's one thing to recognize your internal agenda, but how do you set it aside in the moment? How do you press pause and trade out your agenda, temporarily, to focus on your partner?

Consider a transitional ritual that helps you reset. It could be as simple as taking three deep breaths, putting your phone on silent, or changing into comfortable clothes before engaging with your partner. This creates a mental pause and helps you show up more present.

Cultivate Curiosity

Instead of worrying about saying or doing the "right" thing, start with a curious mindset. Ask yourself, *What's really going on in my partner's world right now?* Then, ask them! Genuinely and without judgment. Curiosity naturally shifts your focus from your own thoughts to their experiences, making it easier to connect.

Curiosity isn't about interrogation. It's about discovery. It invites your partner to share their feelings, thoughts, and needs in a way that feels safe and valued. A simple question like "What's been on your mind today?" or "How did that make you feel?" can open doors to deeper conversations that put the focus on them.

Build a Boundary

Sometimes, distractions steal our attention because we haven't set a boundary. Karolyn and I, for example, have long held a boundary around our dinner table: no multitasking, no TV, and no phone calls. It's a time we count on for giving and getting each other's full attention, uninterrupted by the noise of life.

Where can you set a boundary that creates a full-focus zone for your relationship? Maybe it's a long walk where you leave your phone behind. Maybe it's a commitment to no screens during your shared morning coffee. Perhaps it's as simple as a little check-in time once the kiddos are in bed. The key is to create intentional moments where distractions are minimized and your attention is fully on each other.

Boundaries say: *This time is sacred, and you are my priority.* It's a surefire way to set aside a self-focused agenda.

Invite Feedback

This one takes courage: Ask your partner how you're doing when it comes to giving them your attention. It's not just about checking in. It's about gaining a new perspective on your ability to focus on them instead of your own agenda. Essentially, it's another way of getting a glimpse into their love tank level—but from a different vantage point.

Here's why this matters: Your partner is likely to see you more objectively than you see yourself. If you need convincing, consider a study of three hundred married couples where both partners rated their own and their partner's level of emotions, like anger and argumentativeness.[6] The results? People's self-ratings were significantly less accurate than their spouse's ratings of them. We often struggle to see ourselves as clearly as those closest to us do.

So, if you're feeling strong (and a little brave), give it a shot. Ask your partner questions like, "Do you feel like I'm giving you enough of my attention lately?" or "Is there anything I could do better to make you feel more loved?" Their answers might surprise you—and give you invaluable insight into how to grow closer.

Major on Grace, Not Guilt

Never confuse true love with self-denial. Every so often, we encounter someone who believes self-sacrifice itself is the ultimate goal. It's not. True love doesn't require you to abandon your own needs or well-being for the sake of your partner. In fact, constantly denying yourself can lead to resentment, burnout, and an imbalance that undermines the very relationship you're trying to nurture.

As the greatest love poem reminds us, even the most extravagant sacrifices (e.g., giving your body to be burned) can lack true love. Genuine love isn't measured by the size of the sacrifice but by the heart behind the action. It's the intentional, thoughtful choices to prioritize your partner's needs without erasing your own that create meaningful, lasting connection.

One More Question

How are you doing when it comes to setting aside your own agenda to be fully present and attentive to your partner? Poor? Average? Above average?

We're serious. How would you answer the question? We want you to really think about that.

It wouldn't surprise us if you said "above average." Why? Because we know a bit about human nature. And most of us, most of the time, think we're actually better at relationships than we really are.

We (Les and Leslie) demonstrate this phenomenon every autumn in one of our relationships courses at the university. We administer a simple survey to our two hundred students where they evaluate their interpersonal abilities. In other words, they rank, relative to their peers, how well they get along with others.

We collect the information, tabulate the results and display it on the screen. The results are predictable. All of them, every single one, see themselves as "above average." They can't help but laugh out loud as they see the results.

"Isn't it amazing," Les says, tongue-in-cheek, "that in this class of two hundred students we lucked out by having *everyone* be above average?" They laugh more.

Then we reveal on the screen another tidbit from our survey: An astounding 25 percent see themselves in the top 1 percent in terms of their ability to get along with others. This time, the students don't laugh—they gasp.

How is it that fifty students out of two hundred see themselves in the upper echelons of interpersonal savviness, the top 1 percent, compared to their peers? You know the answer. It's more satisfying to believe good things about ourselves than to face the truth.

This chapter was dedicated to facing a hard truth: We humans are compulsively distracted by our own agendas. We carry them everywhere—into conversations, interactions, and even moments meant to show love. Whether it's the constant noise of daily life, unresolved wounds from the past, or an all-consuming project, our self-focus has a way of quietly taking center stage.

But recognizing this truth is the first step to overcoming it. By naming your agenda, cultivating curiosity, building boundaries, and inviting feedback, you can begin to shift the focus. Love languages require presence, attention, and a willingness to prioritize the person in front of you over the distractions within you. And remember, it's not about being above average—it's about being intentional.

YOUR TURN

What's one actionable insight you gained from this chapter about how you might set aside your agenda, momentarily, to give your full attention to your partner?

PART TWO

THE SOLUTION

Love is a delicate dance of emotion and intention.
The journey to fluency begins with unlocking
the depths of your own heart,
deciphering the unique rhythm of
your partner's needs,
and mastering the tools to build an unshakable
bridge between the two.

CHAPTER 4

Listening Between the Lines of Love

The grand ballroom of the White House shimmered under the glow of chandeliers, a place alive with the hum of polite conversation and the gentle clink of champagne glasses. It was yet another evening reception hosted by Franklin D. Roosevelt, an endless parade of well-dressed guests eager to shake the president's hand, exchange a perfunctory pleasantry, and move on. Roosevelt, the consummate charmer, wore his trademark grin—a smile that had disarmed critics and rallied a nation. But tonight, that grin concealed a private frustration: No one, it seemed, was really listening. The endless procession of nods and empty smiles made even the most powerful man in the room feel, for a moment, invisible.

So with a glint of mischief in his eye, FDR decided to test his suspicion. As the next guest approached, he extended his hand, leaned in, and said, with the warmth of a practiced host, "I murdered my grandmother this morning." The guest, nodding vacantly, replied, "Marvelous, Mr. President," already glancing past him to the next handshake.

Amused, Roosevelt repeated the phrase with each new arrival: "I murdered my grandmother this morning." Over and over, the responses came: "How delightful!" "Wonderful, Mr. President!" The absurdity was almost too much to bear. Roosevelt suppressed a chuckle, feeling as though he were an actor in a surreal comedy, delivering a punchline no one cared to hear.

Finally, a foreign diplomat approached. After the same outrageous statement, he paused, leaned in slightly, and with a sly grin replied, "Well, I'm sure she had it coming." Roosevelt's laugh erupted, genuine and unrestrained—a break in the monotony of rehearsed pleasantries. For the first time that evening, someone had not just heard him but engaged with him. It was a small act of listening, but it cut through the polished veneer of polite society and left an impression far deeper than the hundreds of empty exchanges that had come before.

Later that evening, Roosevelt reflected on the moment. The humor lingered, but so did a deeper truth: listening is rare. In its absence, even the most seen person in the room can feel invisible. But when someone listens—truly listens—it is an act of connection and care.

This story, apocryphal or not, carries a lesson as timeless as it is urgent: true listening is astonishingly rare. In a world where so much of our communication is fueled by preoccupation and self-focus, intentional engagement with another's words, emotions, and unspoken needs has become rare indeed. Most of us listen with the intent to reply, not to understand. And in doing so, we miss the opportunity of speaking the love language that matters most.

Listening with a Third Ear

When someone truly listens to us, it feels like stepping out of a storm into a warm, quiet room. The chaos of the world—its judgments, distractions, and noise—fades away, leaving only the presence of someone who sees us, not just at the surface but at our core. David Brooks calls it "beholding" another person.

And famed psychoanalyst Theodor Reik called it "listening with a third ear," the kind of listening that tunes in not only to what is being said but also to what is left unsaid.

Do you know the experience? It's as though someone is holding a mirror to your thoughts, reflecting not just what you've said but what you've struggled to articulate. Their attentiveness creates a space where you feel safe to be yourself, to lay bare your dreams and insecurities without fear of being dismissed or misunderstood. It is one of the most profound gifts someone can offer because, in a world full of fleeting interactions, to be truly listened to is to feel truly loved.

This kind of listening transforms communication into connection. It goes beyond observing words to noticing tone, picking up on patterns, and perceiving the emotions often left unspoken. It's not just an intellectual exercise. It creates a physical release as well. It feels like a deep exhale after holding your breath for too long. Shoulders drop. The tightness in your chest eases. You no longer have to fight to explain yourself or prove your worth. In the quiet of another's focused attention, you find clarity—not just about what you're saying but about who you are. And who is that? A person who is seen, valued, and loved.

Why Love Languages Require Listening

To truly speak someone's love language, you must first listen to understand. Why? Because love is not simply an expression but a translation. It is not enough to know the grammar of gifts or the syntax of touch. Fluency requires a deep and curious knowledge of the person you want to love. As chapter 5 of *The 5 Love Languages* reiterates, "A relationship calls for empathetic listening with a view to understanding the other person's thoughts, feelings, and desires."[7]

If we don't listen, our attempts to speak another's love language risk becoming hollow gestures—like giving someone flowers when they're allergic or planning a surprise party for an introvert. Without the insight that listening provides, we end up projecting our own preferences or assumptions onto our partner, offering what *we* think they want rather than what they genuinely need. It's the relationship equivalent of confidently singing the wrong lyrics to their favorite song—not just off-key, but missing the point entirely. Listening ensures we're actually hitting the right notes.

Consider Sarah and Ben. They'd been married for five years when Sarah started feeling disconnected. She knew Ben loved her and Ben thought he was speaking Sarah's love language: words of affirmation. And on the surface, he was. "You're amazing," he'd say with all the enthusiasm of someone reading the back of a cereal box. But to Sarah, his words felt generic and almost rehearsed, like he had a mental checklist: *Compliment wife? Check. Done for the day.* She craved something deeper—a connection that made her feel truly seen, not just vaguely appreciated.

What Ben didn't realize was that Sarah needed words rooted in understanding, not just routine compliments. She had been struggling with self-doubt at work, dropping hints about feeling overwhelmed. Ben focused on offering affirmations in general. He missed hearing the fear and vulnerability in her tone. If he had been listening with his "third ear," he might have picked up on her deeper needs and said something like, "I know how hard you're working, and I see how much you're giving. Your team is lucky to have you."

Because Ben wasn't attuned to Sarah's unspoken emotions, his words fell flat—even though his intentions were good. Listening for understanding would have helped Ben tune into Sarah's deeper feelings and vulnerabilities. Without this level of listening, love risks becoming surface-level, missing the opportunity for meaningful connection.

Love languages aren't about what feels natural to us. They're about what resonates deeply with the person we care about. And we can only discover their lexicon of love by truly listening.

You Can't Speak Love Until You Listen

Every love language requires listening to unlock its full potential. It's not enough to simply know your partner values acts of service or quality time, you need to understand *how* they experience that love in ways that feel personal and meaningful to them.

Listening is what helps you move from guessing to knowing. It allows you to pick up on the nuances of their preferences, notice what they value most, and respond in ways that resonate deeply. Each love language calls for its own kind of listening—whether it's tuning in to unspoken needs, noticing subtle hints, or being fully present in the moment. By listening with care and curiosity, you can speak love in any language and speak it in a way that truly connects.

Listening to Words of Affirmation

For someone whose love language is words of affirmation, listening means understanding the specific kinds of words that uplift them. Surface-level praise doesn't cut it—"Nice shirt!" isn't exactly going to melt their heart. Instead, listen to what they truly value. Pay attention to what they talk about with pride or where they seem to seek validation. Do they light up when you acknowledge their hard work, their kindness, or their creativity? Are they looking for encouragement in areas where they feel insecure? By listening closely, you can tailor your affirmations to speak directly to their heart, offering words that feel genuine and deeply meaningful. For someone who values words of affirmation, it's not just what you say—it's that you've listened in a way that makes them feel seen.

Listening to Quality Time

Being fully present in the moment. That's what listening looks like in this language. Distractions like checking your phone or letting your mind wander during a shared activity can feel like rejection to them. Listening in the context of quality time means tuning in with your whole being, showing them they have your undivided attention. It's about engaging deeply in the experience, whether it's a conversation, a walk, or simply sitting together. By listening attentively, you're saying, *I value this moment with you, and you are worth my focus.* For a person who treasures quality time, this kind of intentional presence communicates love far more than the words themselves.

Listening to Receiving Gifts

Here, listening means paying close attention to your loved one's preferences, desires, and the little things that light them up. It's not about the cost of the gift, as you already know, but the "listening ear" behind it. Listening in this context requires you to notice the subtle hints they drop—like mentioning a favorite book they've been meaning to read, admiring a particular kind of flower, or expressing excitement about a local shop they love. It's about understanding what matters to them and using that knowledge to choose a gift that feels personal and meaningful. By listening carefully, you demonstrate that you truly know them and have put thought into making them feel valued.

Listening to Acts of Service

For someone whose love language is acts of service, listening means understanding what kinds of actions truly matter to them. It's not about guessing or doing what you *think* would help. It's about paying attention to what they express as needs, frustrations, or things that would make their life easier. Do they often mention feeling overwhelmed by certain chores or stress over specific responsibilities? Have they hinted at tasks they struggle to find time for? Listening in this context means tuning in to their unspoken priorities and responding with thoughtful actions that address those specific needs. When you listen well and act on what you hear, it communicates love in a way that feels tangible and deeply supportive to someone who values acts of service.

Listening to Physical Touch

For someone whose love language is physical touch, listening involves being attuned to how, when, and where they feel most comforted or connected through your touch. It's about noticing their body language, tone, and subtle cues that signal their needs. Do they lean into you during a quiet moment, reach for your hand during a stressful day, or seem to crave a hug after a long time apart? Listening in this context also means respecting their boundaries and preferences—understanding what kinds of touch are meaningful and when they are most receptive to it. By tuning in with care and sensitivity, you can offer physical connection that feels natural and deeply loving.

Listening is the thread that weaves all five love languages into meaningful connection. It turns acts of service into thoughtful gestures, words of affirmation into genuine encouragement, and quality time into shared moments of presence. It helps you choose gifts that feel personal and offer physical touch that comforts and connects. When you listen—really listen—you gain the insight to love in ways that resonate deeply with the person you care about. Love languages without listening are like speaking without understanding. Listening is what ensures your love is felt, not just expressed. Listening is what enables you to become fluent in love.

The Best Way to Be a Bad Listener

You know the experience. You're talking, but the other person is only half there. They nod absently, toss in the occasional "mm-hmm," or glance at their phone mid-sentence. On the surface, they seem engaged, but you can feel it—their mind is somewhere else. And honestly, at that point, you probably wish you were too.

When someone is being a bad listener, it's as if they're saying: *Your words don't matter enough to merit my full attention.* Bad listening has a way of making you feel like background noise in someone else's internal monologue.

Of course, this is bound to happen from time to time. Loose ends pull at our focus. A distraction blurs the moment. But when this becomes a pattern—when inattentiveness feels like the default—the person speaking begins to feel like an afterthought, their words lost in the haze of preoccupation. This kind of faux listening—nodding along, offering noncommittal responses, or glancing at your phone—may seem harmless, but, in fact, it creates a chasm of disconnection.

A pattern of pretending to listen is a failure to honor another person. In fact, pretending to listen when you're not truly engaged is one of the most subtle yet profound forms of disrespect. It sends an unspoken message that the other person's words, emotions, and presence are not worth your time.

Over time, this behavior erodes trust and intimacy, as the person learns they cannot rely on you to hold space for their thoughts and feelings. Preoccupation is the silent thief of connection. It sneaks into conversations, pulling our attention away from the person we love and toward our own swirling thoughts, worries, or distractions. It's the mental noise that keeps us from hearing not just the words being spoken but the emotions and needs behind them.

Preoccupation makes us appear present while being miles away, leaving the other person feeling unseen and unheard. Preoccupation is what makes us a bad listener. True listening requires more than being fully present. It requires curiosity.

The Only Way to Be a Good Listener

Listening is more than a skill. It's a posture—a way of being wholly interested in the other person. It's about leaning in with genuine care. It means setting aside your own agendas, momentarily, to fully engage. It's a choice to be present. When you adopt this posture, listening becomes more than something you do—it becomes part of who you are in the relationship.

So how do you do it? How can you dramatically increase the odds of being a good listener? Our answer is found in one word: *curiosity*.

Curiosity keeps you from making assumptions or rushing to conclusions—it urges you to ask questions, lean into their perspective, and explore the deeper layers of their heart. When curiosity guides your listening, it becomes natural to set aside distractions and give your full attention. It inoculates you from preoccupation.

Curiosity is the essence of being a good listener. It's what caused naturalist Henry David Thoreau to say, "The greatest compliment that was ever paid me was when one asked me what I thought, and attended to my answer."[8] When someone shows a curious interest in what we think, feel, or experience, it validates our worth and deepens the connection between us.

Curiosity isn't complicated. It's simple. It looks like this:

Jordan: "I don't know, I've just been feeling really off at work lately."
Lilia: "Off? What do you mean by that? Like, overwhelmed or something else?"

Jordan: "Kind of overwhelmed, yeah. But it's more like . . . I'm not sure I'm making the kind of impact I want to."

Lilia: "That sounds tough. When you say 'impact,' what does that look like for you? What do you wish was different?"

Jordan: (pauses, then exhales) "I guess I want to feel like the work I'm doing matters, you know? Like it's making a difference."

Lilia: "That makes so much sense. You're someone who really cares about meaning and it sounds like that's what's missing right now. Is there a part of your job that you think could bring that back?"

Jordan: (smiles slightly) "Yeah . . . I think there is. I just haven't let myself go for it because I've been stuck in little tasks. Talking about it now, though, it feels like maybe I should."

Curiosity transforms listening from a passive act into an active pursuit of understanding. It drives us to ask meaningful questions and lean into the conversation. Through curiosity, listening becomes a gift of genuine presence, reminding the other person that their thoughts and feelings truly matter. In short, curiosity is what breathes life into speaking anyone's love language.

The Most Important Question You'll Ever Ask

Since curiosity is essential for connection—and vital to speaking love languages with fluency—it deserves a little more attention. In fact, we want you to know how to cultivate curiosity in an instant. We want to equip you with a single practice that nearly guarantees you'll take on the posture of listening with finesse.

It has to do with the most important question you'll ever ask. Ready? It's called "the follow-up question." Research underscores the pivotal role of follow-up questions in fostering curiosity and conversational understanding. A study highlighted in *Wired* reveals that individuals who consistently ask follow-up questions—those that delve deeper into a topic previously mentioned—are perceived as more likable and attentive.

Imagine a conversation that feels effortless, like a river flowing smoothly, carrying you deeper into someone's world. That's the power of a follow-up question. It's the quiet invitation to go further, to uncover more, to linger just a little longer in the space of shared understanding.

A follow-up question is like opening a door that the other person didn't even realize was there. When your partner mentions they're feeling overwhelmed at home, the easy response might be, "I'm sorry you're feeling that way." But the follow-up, "What's been weighing on you the most?" turns the moment into something more intimate. It draws them out, making them feel seen, heard, and worth knowing. Follow-up questions take conversations from the surface—where it's safe and routine—to a place where emotions and stories come alive. They show you care enough to dive deeper, to lean in, to say without words, "I'm here, and I want to know more."

The beauty of a follow-up question is its subtlety. It doesn't demand or pry. It invites. It leaves room for reflection, for honesty, for vulnerability. When you ask one, you can feel the shift in the conversation—the way someone's tone softens as they realize they're truly being listened to.

In these moments, the art of curiosity transforms from a mental exercise to an emotional connection, turning a simple exchange into something unforgettable. If you want to become a masterful listener, start by asking: *What comes next?* The follow-up is where the heart of the conversation begins.

Listening—truly listening—is the quiet art that animates each of the five love languages. It's the bridge between what we intend and what the other person actually feels. When we set aside our preoccupations and approach with genuine curiosity, when we lean in and ask the kind of follow-up questions that invite someone to open up, we are making a declaration: *You matter.*

To listen between the lines of love is to hear more than words—it is to hear the unspoken heart behind them. In a world saturated with noise and distraction, listening is a radical act. It is the one thing that cuts through the chaos to deliver a message everyone, regardless of their love language, longs to receive: *You are seen. You are heard. You are loved.*

CHAPTER 5

Loving with Your Head as Well as Your Heart

"Before you leave this auditorium, we have a gift for you," Les and I (Leslie) sometimes dream of saying to the audience at one of our marriage seminars. "On a table in the foyer, you'll find a small spray bottle. Inside is something extraordinary—empathy. One spritz brings instant understanding at the deepest levels."

Can you imagine? Couples wouldn't even wait until they're home. They'd be spraying each other with empathy mist before they reached their cars in the parking lot. All across the lot, you'd see misunderstandings melting away in an instant, as if they were never there. Frustrations would be replaced by harmony. You'd see hugs between partners who had barely been holding hands moments before. Not only that, you'd begin hearing laughter where there used to be grumbling. Words of affirmation would flow freely, thoughtful acts of service would come naturally, and touch would feel comforting again. In short, if you listened carefully, you might actually hear hundreds of love tanks filling up simultaneously.

Empathy does that. It's a wonder. It dissolves tension, builds understanding, creates intimacy, and soothes the rough edges of even the most challenging conversations. It transforms criticism into curiosity, defensiveness into openness, and distance into closeness. And it paves the way for becoming fluent in any love language.

How much would you pay for such a miracle? Twenty dollars? Two hundred? Two thousand? The truth is, no price could ever reflect its value. If this magical mist existed, it wouldn't be sold at the corner drugstore. It would be kept in a vault, accessible only to the world's most discerning hearts.

But here's the thing: It's readily available to anyone. Empathy doesn't come in a spray bottle, of course. It's not an aerosol can you could grab on your way out the door. And yet, the magic of empathy is real. It empowers every effort to speak your partner's love language—not just in theory, but in a way that transforms and endures.

Empathy converts a common chore into a loving act of service. It turns words of affirmation into lifelines of love. It makes quality time rich with heartfelt connection, physical touch warm with emotional comfort, and a thoughtful gift an unmistakable symbol of profound care. Empathy isn't just a magical mist—it's the secret to filling your partner's love tank to the brim.

What's Empathy?

In 1855, when poet Walt Whitman wrote his masterwork, *Leaves of Grass*, he said: "I do not ask the wounded person how he feels, I myself become the wounded person."[9] That's empathy. It's imagining life in someone else's skin. It's wearing their shoes. Seeing through their eyes. Empathy is understanding your partner's feelings, desires, ideas, struggles, insecurities, motivations, and actions at a meaningful level.

Dictionary.com defines empathy as "identification with . . . the emotions, thoughts, or attitudes of another."[10] But what it doesn't tell you is how easily empathy can be mistaken for much less. And it doesn't tell you that empathy requires two sides.

Here's the secret most miss: Empathy calls for loving your partner with both your head and heart, concurrently. Most of us do one or the other pretty well. We either feel our partner's emotions with our heart (we sympathize), or we try to solve their problem with our head (we analyze). To do both can be a challenge. But that's what empathy requires: your head and your heart.

Analyzing with Your Head

Some of us are prone to use our head over our heart. Imagine this: Your partner comes to you, visibly upset, saying, "I had the worst day at work. My boss criticized my project in front of the whole team."

Your first instinct? To put on your problem-solving hat. "Well, did you explain why you made those decisions? Maybe your boss was just having a bad day. You shouldn't take it personally."

You're offering what seems like a logical perspective. But while you're busy solving the problem in your head, your partner is still stuck in their heart, feeling hurt and unseen. It happens every time we analyze more than sympathize.

Early on in our marriage, I (Les) would say something like this to Leslie: "If you didn't get so emotional about this problem you might see that it's not that bad." I learned long ago that's not empathy. And in most cases it's not helpful. As Leslie used to remind me, "I don't need you to fix it. I just need you to feel it with me."

Sympathizing with Your Heart

In the early days of aviation, pilots used a descriptive phrase: "Flying by the seat of your pants." Before instruments for aerial navigation were available, the only guide was the pilot's own sense of movement. If he felt pressure on the seat of his aircraft, it probably meant he was ascending. And if he felt weightless, the plane was probably descending. This way of flying, of course, was not at all reliable. Men died because their feelings played tricks on their judgment.

Feelings can be just as deadly when they are the sole instrument for navigating your relationship. And if you're a hard-core sympathizer, you're probably blind to the danger. What you don't realize is that your sympathetic style causes you to jump to conclusions. You may see signs of disapproval from your partner where they don't exist. Or you will tend to project your own feelings onto your spouse before analyzing the situation to see if those feelings are even accurate.

When our partner shares something vulnerable or challenging, our response often comes from the head, the heart, or a combination of both. Each has its impact, but only one leads to true empathy. Here's how these responses play out:

- **Analyzing with Your Head:** "If you just approached this more logically, you'd see it's not such a big deal."
- **Sympathizing with Your Heart:** "I'm so sorry you're feeling this way—it must be really hard for you."
- **Empathizing with Your Head and Heart:** "I can see why this is so tough for you—help me understand more about how you're feeling and what you need right now."

You get the point. Like two wings of an airplane, empathy requires both your head and your heart, both analyzing and sympathizing, to get off the ground.

How to Walk in Your Partner's Shoes

Empathy begins with a willingness to step out of your own perspective and into your partner's. But this isn't about abandoning your feelings or suppressing your thoughts—it's about creating space for theirs. Walking in your partner's shoes means imagining what it's like to be them, not just in general, but in the specific moment they're experiencing.

Start by asking yourself, *What might they be feeling right now?* For example, if your partner comes home frustrated after a long day, resist the urge to fix their mood or dismiss their feelings. Instead, reflect: *If I had their boss, their workload, or their day, how would I feel?* Just that moment of consideration can shift your mindset from problem-solving to understanding.

But empathy doesn't stop at imagining. It involves engaging—asking questions like, "Can you help me understand what's been weighing on you?" or "What would make you feel supported right now?" These questions aren't designed to give you answers to fix a problem, they're designed to open a door to connection. When your partner senses that you're genuinely curious about their world, they feel valued and understood, and that's when love flows.

As you practice walking in your partner's shoes, remember that this isn't a mental exercise to tick off a list—it's the heart of becoming fluent in their love language. When you understand what fills their love tank, you're better equipped to pour into it. Maybe they've been craving acts of service because their life feels overwhelming, or words of affirmation because they're struggling with self-doubt. Empathy gives you the insight you need to not just speak their love language but to speak it with their personal dialect.

True Empathy Requires Intention

Empathy doesn't happen by accident. It's not something you stumble into or effortlessly develop—it's something you choose, moment by moment. While emotions can pull us toward sympathy and logic can push us toward analysis, empathy requires conscious effort. It's about intentionally shifting your focus from your own perspective to your partner's, not because it's easy, but because it's worth it.

Why does intention matter? Because empathy, while powerful, can be fleeting without it. In the heat of an argument or the busyness of life, it's easy to default to self-centered habits—to defend, to dismiss, or to assume. Intentionality is what helps you pause, reflect, and take the next step toward understanding. It's the bridge between knowing empathy is valuable and actually practicing it.

Being intentional with empathy means choosing to listen fully, without strategizing your next rebuttal. It means asking thoughtful questions, even when it feels easier to make assumptions. And it means acting on what you've learned about your partner, whether that's offering comfort, encouragement, or support in their specific love language.

Empathy thrives when paired with intentionality. Together, they create a powerful dynamic that not only builds connection but sustains it. That's why the relationship between empathy and intentionality is at the heart of what it means to be fluent in love.

Consider the varying combinations of empathy and intention:

INTENTIONALITY	Low EMPATHY	High EMPATHY
High	***Frustrated***	***Fluent***
Low	***Frozen***	***Faltering***

Faltering: Empathy Without Intention

- This person knows their partner's love language but isn't speaking it.
- They notice when their partner's love tank is running low but doesn't take steps to fill it.

- Their check-ins with their partner, if they happen, tend to be sporadic or surface-level, lacking follow-through.
- Their partner's love tank runs on reserves or even fumes.

Frustrated: Intention Without Empathy

- This person is trying hard to speak their partner's love language but they're not quite getting it.
- Their actions feel busy but miss the emotional connection their partner craves.
- Their check-ins often focus on actions they think their partner might appreciate, rather than exploring their partner's real emotional needs.
- Their partner's love tank is receiving the wrong fuel.

Frozen: No Empathy or Intention

- This person is not interested in trying to speak their partner's love language.
- This person may not even realize their partner has a love tank or that it needs filling.
- They rarely, if ever, check in with their partner, assuming everything is fine or avoiding the potential discomfort of the answer.
- Their partner's love tank is bone dry.

Fluent: Empathy and Intention

- This person has a command of their partner's love language (as well as their dialect) and speaks it with eloquence.
- This person proactively anticipates their partner's needs, often filling their love tank before it even runs low.
- Their check-ins are thoughtful and specific, often leading to intentional actions that align with their partner's love language.
- Their partner's love tank is often full to the brim.

The combination of empathy and intentionality creates a way of understanding how we show up in our relationships. Whether we're in the **Fluent** quadrant, creating deep connections through understanding and action, or navigating the **Faltering**, **Frustrated**, or **Frozen** zones, these states aren't fixed. Life's stresses, distractions, and challenges can pull us out of one quadrant and into another, sometimes without us realizing it. The good news is that empathy and intentionality are a choice. With self-awareness and a decision to change, we can instantly begin moving toward fluency.

Rachel sat in my office, tears spilling down her cheeks. "Every time I open up about something that's bothering me," she said, "he says the same thing—'I'm so sorry, Honey.' He just repeats it. Over and over again. But what I really want is for him to say, 'Tell me about it.' I want him to show interest—to try and understand why I'm so upset."

Rachel wasn't asking for a fix. She wasn't even asking for advice. She was longing for empathy—a desire to feel seen and heard. But her husband, while well-meaning, was offering sympathy instead. He was offering a phrase, when what she needed was presence.

What Rachel longed for was someone to step into her shoes—to say, "Help me understand what you're feeling. I want to see this the way you see it." And if he had truly listened, she might have felt safe enough to say it all. Only then—after feeling understood—would his words of comfort have landed differently. Perhaps he could have said, "Wow. Now I can see why you're so frustrated. Is there anything I can do that would help?" Maybe she would have had a suggestion. Or maybe she would've said, "Honestly, no—but it helps so much just knowing you get it."

It Never Fails

When we set aside our own agenda to truly see, hear, and feel another's, we create space in our soul for love. Empathy is love in action. It lifts us outside ourselves. It helps us see beyond the normal range of human vision—and over walls of resentment and barriers of betrayal. Love rises above the petty demands and conflicts of life and inspires our spirit to give without getting. As the famous "love chapter" of the Bible says: "Love never fails." And neither does empathy.

How can this be? Is anything truly fail-proof?

Empathy never fails because it aligns us with the heart of love—patience, kindness, humility, respect, selflessness, forgiveness, composure, forgiveness, truth, protection, trust, hope, and perseverance. Empathy empowers all of these.

Even in the face of rejection, misunderstanding, or imperfection, empathy has the power to soften hearts, open doors, and plant seeds of healing. When we choose empathy, we choose to rise above fear and pride. We choose to love.

Empathy never fails because it's not about outcomes. It's about presence. It's about showing up for the person you love and speaking their love language, whether or not they meet you halfway. When we live this way—with our head and heart working together—we find that empathy becomes the highest expression of love. And love, as we know, never fails.

YOUR TURN

Where do you land on the diagram that combines empathy and intention and what will you take from this chapter to help you become more fluent in love?

CHAPTER 6

How Personality Colors the Conversation

One of the questions I have often received about *The 5 Love Languages* is: "How does personality factor into it?" While I mentioned personality differences in the original book, I had never done a deep dive to show how they interface with each of the five love languages.

But no longer.

Les and Leslie have revealed exactly how personality factors into each of the five love languages. As we worked together on the 5 Love Languages Premium Assessment a few years ago, they began to show me how our hardwiring, or personality traits, shape how we hear words of affirmation, what we want from quality time, the way we interpret the meaning of a gift, how an act of service can resonate most, and even the kind of physical touch that feels most meaningful.

Their insights were both eye-opening and deeply practical, helping me see how personality nuances add a whole new dimension to understanding and speaking the love languages.

In this chapter, you'll discover how personality isn't just a backdrop—it's a vital part of how we express and experience love. And while there are unlimited personality variables worth exploring, we are focusing on four that stand out from the pack in terms of how they interact with the love languages.

Each is an established and thoroughly researched set of dichotomies, two ends on a continuum:

- Introversion vs. Extroversion
- Cautious vs. Curious
- Carefree vs. Dependable
- Cool vs. Warm

We've charted the way for you to understand each of these important dimensions of personality and how they influence love. Quite literally. You'll find a fascinating chart for each of these dimensions in the pages to come. You don't necessarily need to read every word of each chart. Focus on the love language that matters most to your partner. That's the part of the chart where you'll find the most value.

We believe the insights you're about to get in this chapter aren't just the "answer" to how personality traits play a role in the five love languages—they're a game changer.

By recognizing your partner's personality, you can tailor your loving efforts with greater precision. Whether your partner is naturally introverted or extroverted, cautious or curious, carefree or dependable, cool or warm, these traits shape the way love lands in their heart, and yours too.

Introversion vs. Extroversion

This is one of the most well-known dimensions of personality, shaping how individuals recharge and connect with the world. Understanding these tendencies is more than just personality trivia—it's a key to unlocking how your partner experiences love most naturally.

Introversion	Extroversion
Prefers quiet and reflective environments	Draws energy from dynamic and lively interactions
Enjoys deep one-on-one conversations	Enjoys the vibrancy of group conversations
Recharges by spending time alone	Recharges through shared experiences
Values thoughtfulness over spontaneity	Leans into spontaneity and quick decisions
Processes internally	Processes outwardly
May need time before addressing conflict	Seeks resolution through immediate dialogue

Which one of these two categories best describes you? How about your partner? These are important questions because each type has their own unique way of approaching connection when it comes to giving and receiving love. The better you understand this dimension of your partner's personality, the easier it becomes to speak their love language.

In general, introverts experience love best in quieter, more intimate ways with low-key gestures and private moments they can savor. Over-the-top gestures might feel overwhelming or insincere to them. Extroverts, on the other hand, experience love more openly and boldly with grander gestures that have more lively energy. They generally feel at ease showing love and affection in social gatherings. Of course, your partner may be somewhere in the middle, a blend of both.

Let's compare and contrast how introversion and extroversion influence each of the five love languages with a specific example and why it works.

	Introverts	Extroverts
Words of Affirmation	Writing a heartfelt letter or leaving a Post-it note on their mirror with a compliment *This allows them to process the message privately and revisit it when they need it*	Praising them in front of their friends or coworkers, or enthusiastic compliments *They enjoy public affirmation and the energetic exchange of positive words*
Quality Time	Planning a quiet evening at home watching a movie or taking a serene walk in nature *They feel connected through undistracted, one-on-one moments*	Organizing a group outing or attending a lively event together, like a concert or comedy show *They thrive on shared experiences that involve energy, interaction, and activity*
Receiving Gifts	Choosing a thoughtful, meaningful gift that reflects their personal interests, like a book by their favorite author *They value the thought behind the gift and enjoy reflecting on the meaning privately*	Surprising them with a flashy or fun gift that they can share or show off, like a new gadget or tickets to an event *They enjoy gifts that create excitement and opportunities for engagement*

Acts of Service	Quietly taking care of a task they've been procrastinating on, like organizing a closet or preparing their favorite meal *It demonstrates thoughtfulness without requiring immediate reciprocation*	Completing a task that has a noticeable, immediate impact, like decorating their workspace or preparing for a group gathering *They enjoy acts that support their busy, social lifestyle and can be shared with others*
Physical Touch	Offering a soft, lingering hug or holding hands during a quiet moment *They prefer physical affection that feels intimate and unhurried*	Giving a playful shoulder squeeze or greeting them with an enthusiastic hug in a social setting *They appreciate touch that is spontaneous, energetic, and outwardly expressive*

Susan was sure she was speaking love to Roger when she planned a surprise birthday party for him. She coordinated the whole thing with friends, arranged the food, and carefully kept it under wraps for weeks. On the morning of his birthday, she told Roger she wanted to take him out to dinner that evening to celebrate. So that afternoon, he came home from work expecting a nice evening together—just the two of them.

"I'll drive," Susan said with a smile. "I've got a little surprise."

A short drive later, they pulled up to a friend's house. Roger glanced at her, puzzled. "Why are we stopping here?"

"They just wanted us to swing by so they could say happy birthday," she said casually.

It seemed odd to Roger, but he went along with it. As they stepped inside, thirty people suddenly burst into song: *"Happy Birthday to You!"* Roger was stunned. He smiled, thanked everyone, and did his best to enjoy the moment. The food was great. He had a few good conversations. From the outside, everything went smoothly.

Later, on the drive home, Roger said kindly, "Well, you really surprised me tonight. How long have you been planning this?"

"About six weeks," Susan said, beaming. "I just wanted to do something special because I love you."

Roger smiled and replied, "Thank you, darling. I love you too."

But in his mind, he was thinking, *I would've enjoyed a quiet dinner with you a lot more.*

He genuinely appreciated her effort—but it didn't fill his love tank the way she had hoped. The missing piece? Understanding how Roger's personality shaped the way he received love. He was an introvert, uncomfortable in large social settings—especially when all eyes were on him.

Now that you can see how introversion and extroversion shape the way a person might experience each love language, consider your loved one. Which side of these two columns are they likely to land on? Or are they somewhere in between?

For introverts, love often whispers through quiet moments—a lingering glance, the brush of a hand, or the unspoken comfort of simply being together. For extroverts, love tends to shout with joy—a boisterous laugh, a heartfelt cheer, or the energy of a shared adventure. Love is received differently for each type, and when you consider this part of their personality, you're tuning in to their heart and making a connection that truly resonates.

Cautious vs. Curious

This dimension of personality reflects how we approach new experiences, ideas, and risks. It's asking if you are someone who finds comfort in the familiar, or are you energized by exploring the unknown? Understanding this distinction helps illuminate how your partner navigates life—and love. It's more than just a preference; it's a lens through which they interpret connection and intimacy.

Cautious	Curious
Prefers familiar routines and predictability	Thrives on novelty and new experiences
Carefully weighs risks before taking action	Leaps at opportunities to explore the unknown
Finds satisfaction in incremental progress	Seeks excitement in big, bold leaps forward
Values consistency and reliability	Values flexibility and adaptability
Approaches new ideas with skepticism	Approaches new ideas with enthusiasm
Prefers slow, deliberate decision-making	Embraces spontaneity and quick decision-making

Does your partner tend to play it safe, preferring familiar routines and thoughtful planning? Or are they the type who lights up at the prospect of a new adventure, eager to dive into the unknown? Perhaps they're somewhere in between. Understanding where your partner lands on this spectrum can reveal a lot about how they connect and respond to love.

Cautious individuals often feel most loved when gestures reinforce security and dependability—consistent, predictable acts that demonstrate care. Curious individuals, however, come alive with spontaneity and fresh experiences, finding connection in creativity and bold expressions of love. Both approaches can be meaningful, but knowing which resonates with your partner makes all the difference.

Now, let's take a closer look at how these two tendencies shape each of the five love languages, along with specific examples and why they work.

	Cautious	Curious
Words of Affirmation	Sharing a steady stream of reassuring, thoughtful compliments over time *Dependable affirmations help them build trust*	Surprising them with an unexpected, heartfelt, or unique declaration of love or admiration *They thrive on fresh and creative ways to express words*
Quality Time	Sticking to a familiar routine, like a weekly dinner or an evening walk together *They appreciate predictable moments that feel steady and safe*	Planning a spontaneous day trip or trying a new activity, like kayaking or a cooking class *They enjoy bonding through adventures that break routine and spark excitement*
Receiving Gifts	Giving a practical, thoughtful gift that solves a problem or adds to their comfort (like a back pillow) *They value traditional gifts that demonstrate care*	Surprising them with an unusual, fun gift, something quirky like a personalized puzzle or a unique gadget *They love gifts that feel exciting, playful, or spark curiosity*

Acts of Service	Taking care of routine tasks or planning ahead to reduce stress, like meal prep or taking out the trash *They feel loved through consistent and reliable acts that enhance stability*	Jumping in with a spontaneous act of help, like rearranging a room or brainstorming together *They appreciate acts that feel energetic and engage their sense of possibility and exploration*
Physical Touch	Offering a gentle, reassuring handhold or a steady hug when they're feeling unsure *They prefer touch that feels calm, predictable, and steady*	Surprising them with playful, energetic gestures like a spin hug or a spontaneous cuddle *They enjoy touch that's lively, engaging, and reflects the thrill of the moment*

Bill and Jennifer couldn't have been more different when it came to how they approached the world.

Bill has always been curious. As a kid, he'd wander off the beaten path just to see where it led. As an adult, that same trait shows up in spontaneous ideas, last-minute road trips, and a deep love for the unexpected.

Jennifer, on the other hand, is cautious. She thrives on structure. Her calendar is color-coded. She finds comfort in knowing what's coming and when.

So when Bill blurted out over Friday night dinner, "Hey, let's wake up early and hike Pilot Mountain tomorrow," Jennifer barely looked up from her plate.

"I already have my Saturday planned."

Bill laughed, thinking she just needed a little nudging. "So bump it to next weekend. Come on—sunrise hike, just the two of us!"

What followed wasn't just a disagreement. It was a clash of core temperaments.

Jennifer felt steamrolled—like her carefully laid-out day didn't matter. Bill felt rejected—like his invitation to connect was brushed aside.

Neither of them was wrong. They were simply speaking different languages, shaped by personality.

Bill saw his spontaneity as romantic. Jennifer saw it as disruptive. He felt energized by possibility; she felt safe in predictability. But at the heart of it, both were expressing love—just in very different ways.

Understanding how cautious and curious tendencies influence love languages can offer valuable insight into your partner's world. Does your partner gravitate toward the security of familiar routines, or do they find excitement in the unexpected? Perhaps they embody a bit of both.

For the cautious, love often feels like a steady hand—a thoughtful act, a calm presence, or the quiet reassurance of consistency. For the curious, love is an adventure—an exciting gesture, a creative surprise, or the shared thrill of something new. By recognizing and honoring this aspect of their personality, you're not just more likely to leverage their love language—you're meeting them exactly where they are, in a way that they are sure to feel deeply.

Carefree vs. Dependable

This dimension of personality highlights how people balance structure and spontaneity in their lives. Is your partner someone who thrives on flexibility and living in the moment, or do they feel most secure when plans are made and commitments are honored? These traits shape more than just daily routines—they influence how your partner experiences and expresses love. Recognizing this part of their personality can help you align your gestures with what feels most natural and meaningful to them.

Carefree	Dependable
Embraces flexibility and spontaneity	Thrives on structure and clear plans
Values living in the moment	Values long-term thinking and preparation
Enjoys taking things as they come	Prefers predictable routines and schedules
Comfortable with uncertainty and change	Feels secure when commitments are honored
Approaches decisions casually and intuitively	Approaches decisions carefully
Prioritizes fun and freedom	Prioritizes responsibility and reliability

Is your partner the kind of person who thrives on freedom and spontaneity, embracing life as it comes? Or do they feel most comfortable when everything is thoughtfully planned and well-organized? Maybe they're a mix of both. Again, understanding where they fall on this spectrum can offer valuable insight into how they will best respond to your loving gestures.

Carefree individuals often feel most loved through lighthearted, flexible gestures that celebrate the present moment—unexpected surprises or simple, unstructured quality time. Dependable individuals, on the other hand, are deeply moved by thoughtful, reliable acts that show commitment and care—gestures that bring a sense of stability and follow-through. Neither approach is better, of course. Each simply reflects a unique way of experiencing love.

Let's explore how these two tendencies influence the five love languages, complete with specific examples and why they resonate.

	Carefree	Dependable
Words of Affirmation	A spontaneous, playful compliment, like texting them a sweet message out of the blue *They enjoy affirmations that feel fun and unplanned, matching their love for spontaneity*	Regular, thoughtful affirmations, like a heartfelt note left in the same spot each day *They appreciate affirmations that demonstrate consistency and commitment over time*
Quality Time	Suggesting an impromptu picnic or an unplanned outing to a favorite spot *They feel connected through unstructured, lighthearted moments*	Scheduling a recurring date night or planning a well-organized day together *They value the reliability and intention of dedicated, planned time*
Receiving Gifts	Giving an unexpected gift, like something from a small boutique *They enjoy gifts that feel surprising and one-of-a-kind*	Selecting a meaningful, practical gift, like a high-quality tool they've been needing *They feel loved through gifts that show forethought and usefulness*

Acts of Service	Offering to help spontaneously, like taking over a task they were stressing about last minute *They value spontaneous acts that lighten the mood and bring a sense of freedom or relief*	Following through on planned acts, like organizing a shared calendar or keeping the house tidy consistently *They feel loved when acts of service are dependable and align with their expectations*
Physical Touch	Giving playful and casual touch, like a quick tickle or an unexpected smooch *They appreciate touch that feels lively and in the moment*	Offering steady and comforting touch, like holding their hand or giving a long hug *They prefer touch that conveys stability and reassurance*

Now that you've explored how carefree and dependable tendencies shape the way your loved one may experience their love language, think about how you can apply it. Do they light up when plans go out the window and life takes an unexpected turn, or do they feel most loved when things unfold exactly as expected? Of course, they may very well sit somewhere between these two extremes, combining a need for stability with a touch of spontaneity.

For the carefree, love often feels like a breath of fresh air—a playful surprise, a moment of shared laughter, or a spontaneous adventure that breaks the routine. For the dependable, love feels like a steady presence—planned gestures, reliable acts of service, or the comfort of knowing they can count on you. Again, neither approach is better or worse. They simply reflect different personality types.

Carrie often expressed love in the middle of everyday life. Once, while grocery shopping, she saw the word "sunshine" on a label and burst into song: "You are my sunshine . . ."—right there in the aisle. Brian appreciated the sentiment, but he was more embarrassed than touched. He would've much preferred finding those same words written in a quiet note tucked into his backpack.

If Brian had understood Carrie's personality, he might've even returned the gesture—maybe not with a song, but in his own way.

Cool vs. Warm

This is the last of the four dichotomous trait sets. It has to do with how we approach relationships in general, our emotional connections. Is your partner someone who leads with logic and prefers to keep emotions at a distance, or do they naturally express affinity and affection in their interactions? As always they may be somewhere in between. Understanding where your partner falls on this spectrum can reveal a lot about how they give and receive love—and how you can best connect with them in a way that matters most.

Cool	Warm
Leads with logic and rationality	Leads with emotional connection
Tends to keep emotions private or at a distance	Openly expresses affection and care
Values independence and self-reliance	Values closeness and emotional intimacy
Prefers straightforward, practical interactions	Prefers collaborative, harmonious interactions

May appear reserved or detached	Naturally comforting and supportive
Focuses on problem solving	Focuses on feelings and understanding

Does your partner tend to keep things logical and measured, focusing on solutions rather than emotions? Or are they naturally expressive and tuned in socially, seeking to connect on a deeper emotional level? Of course, they may fall somewhere in between. Recognizing this aspect of your partner's personality is another way to better understand how they navigate love and connection.

For those with a cooler personality, love often feels like steadiness—a practical gesture, a thoughtful act, or a quiet presence that shows care without excess emotion. For those with a warmer personality, love is more openly felt—affectionate words, emotional connection, and gestures that create closeness and harmony. Each approach has its own beauty, and when you honor your partner's style, you're getting closer to speaking their love language in a way that matters to them.

Now, let's explore how cool and warm personalities influence each of the five love languages, with specific examples of what works and why.

	Cool	Warm
Words of Affirmation	A practical compliment about their skills or accomplishments *They appreciate words that are straightforward, grounded in facts*	An emotionally expressive affirmation, like telling them how much they mean to you *They value words that convey warmth and emotional depth*

Quality Time	Spending time together working on a shared project *They feel connected through productive and shared activities*	Engaging in a heartfelt conversation or a cozy evening focused entirely on them *They feel loved when time is spent creating emotional closeness*
Receiving Gifts	Giving a practical, functional gift, like a high-quality tool or a useful device *They appreciate gifts that solve problems or enhance daily life*	Giving a sentimental gift, like a personalized or symbolic keepsake *They value gifts that carry emotional significance and show deep thought*
Acts of Service	Handling practical tasks, like organizing finances or fixing something *They feel loved through efficient, logical support*	Doing something thoughtful that makes their day easier, like cooking their favorite meal *They feel loved when acts of service convey emotional care and attention*
Physical Touch	Offering a brief but intentional touch, like a reassuring pat on the shoulder They appreciate touch that is subtle and purposeful	Expressing affection through warm, lingering touches *They value touch that conveys emotional closeness and comfort*

So, after reviewing this, do you think your partner is more reserved, valuing thinking over feeling, or do they lean into affection and heartfelt moments? Maybe they're a blend of both, balancing logic and emotion in their unique way.

For cooler personalities, love often feels understated and practical. For warmer personalities, love is more about affectionate words, heartfelt actions, and moments of emotional closeness. Both approaches are valid and meaningful, but understanding your partner's natural style helps you better connect and empathize with them.

George was calm, cool, and collected. He didn't ride emotional highs or lows. Whether the day brought good news or bad, he approached life with the same steady logic and matter-of-fact tone. To George, love wasn't something you gushed about—it was something you demonstrated in practical, dependable ways.

So for their first Valentine's Day as a married couple, George gave Rebecca an electric food mixer. A really nice one. Stainless steel. Top of the line.

Rebecca smiled politely. "Thank you," she said. But inside, her heart sank a little.

She wasn't expecting diamonds, but she had imagined something more—well, *romantic.* Flowers. A handwritten card. Maybe dinner by candlelight. Something that said, *I see you. I cherish you.*

To George, the mixer made perfect sense. It was useful. Thoughtful. High quality. A sign that he was paying attention to what they needed. To Rebecca, it felt more like a transaction than a tender moment.

George wasn't trying to be unfeeling—he just naturally leads with logic. He keeps his emotions tucked in and assumes others do too. Rebecca, on the other hand, thrives on emotional connection. For her, warmth isn't optional—it's essential.

That's the difference between a "cool" and "warm" personality.

Cool types often show love through action and problem-solving. Warm types express more affection and emotional resonance.

Both approaches can be meaningful—but only if we learn to see love through our partner's lens.

How's Your Partner Hardwired?

As you've explored these four dimensions of personality—Introversion vs. Extroversion, Cautious vs. Curious, Carefree vs. Dependable, and Cool vs. Warm—we hope you've gained insights into how your partner's personality can shape their experiences of receiving your love.

Take a moment to think about where your partner might land on each of these spectrums. Consider how their personality shows up in your daily interactions, and note where they might land, from your perspective, on each continuum:

Once you've noted their tendencies, ask yourself: How can I tailor my expressions of love to align with what feels most meaningful to them? Of course, this exercise isn't about getting it perfect or making it complicated, it's about learning to love your partner in the way that speaks most deeply to who they are.

What You See vs. Who They Are

Rather than assuming you have your partner completely figured out, approach this exercise with curiosity and humility. Use it as an opportunity to start a conversation: "I think you might be more introverted than extroverted, but I'd love to hear how you see yourself." Or, "I notice you value structure, but do you also like spontaneity?" You may even want to invite them to place themselves on each of the four continuums. The bottom line is to cultivate conversations to better understand their hardwiring. They'll likely do the same with you.

Importantly, remember, this exercise is not about labeling your partner or fitting them neatly into categories. It's about gaining insights that help you connect more deeply, while remaining open to learning more about who they truly are.

One more thing. We feel compelled to remind you that your evaluation of your partner's personality is only as reliable as your perceptions. And while those perceptions can be spot-on, they can also miss the mark. In fact, a Texas A&M University study found that we humans tend to overestimate our ability to accurately judge the complex traits of someone's personality—even when we feel we know them well.[11]

In other words, our assumptions may not align with reality. So don't rely solely on assumptions. Again, chat about how your partner sees themselves. Better yet, invite your partner to join you in taking the 5 Love Languages Premium Assessment. It maps out their personality (and much more) and how their hardwiring shapes the nuances and tendencies of their love language. It's an incredibly powerful tool, offering the clearest way to personalize your understanding of how your partner's personality (as well as your own) interacts with and experiences love. By exploring this together, you'll deepen your connection and pave the way for speaking the love language that matters most—to both of you.

YOUR TURN

How will you adapt your expressions of love to align more closely with your partner's unique personality?

PART THREE

THE TACTICS

Each of the five chapters in Part Three serves as a tailored action plan to help you master the love language that matters most to your partner.

Feel free to jump to the chapters that are most relevant to you.

CHAPTER 7

Words of Affirmation

Speaking Straight to the Heart

Mary glanced at the clock on the wall, its slow tick somehow louder in the silence of the conference room. The equations on the chalkboard behind her felt like a blur now—an exhausting, nerve-wracking blur. She'd just finished presenting her solution to a problem that had stumped her team for weeks, and the room of engineers and mathematicians was quiet.

Too quiet.

Her palms felt damp as she gathered her papers. She told herself not to look at their faces, not to search for signs of approval—or worse, judgment. But she couldn't help it. The supervisor, a stern man with piercing eyes, stood and walked toward her.

"Mrs. Jackson," he began, his tone unreadable. She braced herself, preparing for the critique, for the nitpicking she had come to expect in a workplace where she always felt the need to prove herself.

But then he smiled—a rare, genuine smile. "The way you solved that equation," he said, pausing for a moment as if to let the weight of his words sink in, "it's something only you could have done. Your mind works in a way this team needs."

The room seemed to exhale, and so did Mary. She felt the corners of her mouth lift in an involuntary smile. Those few words didn't just affirm her work—they affirmed her. They silenced the self-doubt that had shadowed her every step at NASA's Langley Research Center, where women like her were often doubted before they even walked through the door, especially in 1958.

Mary Jackson carried those words of affirmation with her for the rest of her career, becoming NASA's first Black female engineer. They didn't just encourage her—they fueled her. Because sometimes, all it takes is a single word of affirmation to change a person's story.

A Quick Review

Words of affirmation is about quality over quantity. It's about saying the right thing in the right way, at the right time. As you learned in chapter 4 of *The 5 Love Languages*, for the person whose heart resonates with this language, hearing affirming words isn't just nice—it's essential to feeling loved and connected.

Ways to Practice **Words of Affirmation**

- *"You handled that conversation with such grace. I'm so proud of how you stood your ground while being kind."*
- *"I noticed how much effort you put into dinner tonight—it was incredible. Thank you for taking care of us like that."*
- *"I know this project at work is tough, but you're the perfect person for it. You've got this!"*
- *"You have such a creative mind—it amazes me how you come up with ideas like that."*
- *"You look absolutely stunning today. I couldn't stop smiling when I saw you."*

Words like these may seem simple, but their impact can be profound for the person with this love language, especially when they're delivered with sincerity and thoughtfulness. For someone who thrives on words of affirmation, these expressions aren't just about the words themselves—they're about the love and care those words represent. As we dive deeper into understanding how to personalize this love language, you'll discover how to move beyond generic compliments and truly speak to the heart of your partner in their own dialect.

Why Affirmation Speaks Straight to the Heart

Words of affirmation meet a deep human need for connection. Everyone benefits from being affirmed, but for some, words resonate on an even deeper level. Growing up in environments where affirmation was either scarce or abundant shapes how we associate words with love. Whether filling a gap or reinforcing a foundation, affirmations make us feel seen, valued, and understood.

Psychologically, people drawn to affirmation are highly attuned to verbal cues and the nuances of language. Attachment theory (which explains how we form emotional bonds) suggests that those with insecure attachments early in their life may seek affirmations to combat feelings of inadequacy. People who grew up with secure attachments rely on them to maintain emotional connection.

Traits like *introversion* can also amplify the impact of affirming words, since these individuals process emotions inwardly. For them, affirming words are not just compliments—they are lifelines that provide emotional security. And traits like *warmth* and *dependability* (described in our previous chapter) thrive in environments rich with verbal appreciation, reinforcing harmony and belonging. In other words, for certain personality types, words of affirmation feel like oxygen to the soul.

When Affirmations Matter Most

Affirming words are powerful all the time, but there are certain moments when they take on extraordinary significance. These are the times when your partner is most in need of reassurance, encouragement, or validation—moments when the right words can make all the difference.

Times of Vulnerability

Words of affirmation are most powerful in moments of vulnerability, insecurity, challenge, or uncertainty. During these times, an affirming word can act as an emotional anchor, providing reassurance and strength when your partner feels emotionally adrift. For example: *"I know this situation feels overwhelming, but I see your strength, and I believe in your ability to get through it."*

For someone whose love language is words of affirmation, silence in these moments can be deafening—leaving them to wonder if they are truly supported or appreciated. When they face a difficult decision, experience a failure, or simply feel unseen, affirmations serve as a lifeline, reminding them of their worth and the steadfastness of your love.

Times of Change

Affirmation is also critical during transitions. Whether it's starting a new job, moving to a new place, or navigating a loss, these seasons can bring feelings of instability. For example: "I'm so impressed by how you're handling this transition—it shows so much courage and grace."

A well-timed affirmation—like acknowledging their courage, recognizing their perseverance, or reminding them of your unwavering support—can provide the grounding they need. Even a simple statement like "I'm proud of how you're handling this" can reinforce their inner strength and affirm your shared commitment to facing challenges together.

Times of Tension

Moments of conflict or disconnection are another time when affirmation is especially needed. When tensions run high, an affirming word can disarm defensiveness and rebuild trust—as long as it's heartfelt. Saying something as simple as, "I know we're not seeing eye to eye, but I respect your perspective," can soften the emotional landscape and pave the way for healing.

For someone who craves affirming words, this kind of gesture communicates, "I'm still with you, even in this." As long as it's genuine, it reassures them that the relationship is stronger than the conflict and worth working through together.

When Not to Be Affirming

While words of affirmation are powerful, there are moments when they can feel insincere, manipulative, or even counterproductive. Knowing when to hold back is as important as knowing when to speak up. Affirmation should always be rooted in truth and authenticity—offering it at the wrong time or for the wrong reasons can undermine its impact.

For example, avoid offering affirmations when they might seem like an attempt to gloss over a serious issue. If your partner is upset or processing hurt, jumping straight to affirmations like "You're amazing; you'll be fine" can come across as dismissive or tone-deaf. Instead, acknowledge their feelings first before offering support. Authentic affirmation must meet your partner where they are, not bypass their reality.

Another moment to tread carefully is during conflict resolution. If affirmations are used to manipulate or pacify your partner into agreeing with your perspective—"You're so smart; I know you'll see it my way"—they lose their genuine meaning and are likely to breed resentment. Affirmation in conflict should build trust, not serve as a tool to win an argument.

How Words of Affirmation Can Get Lost in Translation

Not all affirmations land the way we intend. Even with the best of intentions, our words can sometimes miss the mark, leaving our partner feeling more confused than loved. This happens whenever we fail to consider their unique preferences, context, or emotional needs.

One common issue is offering generic or vague compliments. Saying something like "You're great" or "Good job" might seem affirming, but to someone who thrives on words of affirmation, it can be about as satisfying as being told, "You're my favorite person . . . whose name I can't remember." Without specifics, it can feel hollow or impersonal. For them, it's the details that matter—highlighting exactly what you noticed or why it impressed you turns a "meh" compliment into one that really lands.

Another way affirmations can miss the mark is when they clash with your partner's emotional state. Telling someone "You're amazing at handling stress" while they're visibly overwhelmed might feel less like support and more like you're narrating a bad reality show.

Timing and tone matter as much as the words themselves. Instead, try meeting them where they are with something like, "I can see how much you're carrying right now, and I want you to know I've got your back." This kind of affirmation not only acknowledges their feelings but also reinforces your belief in their strength—without sounding out of touch.

Finally, affirmations can lose their impact when paired with actions that contradict them. Saying "I appreciate you" but failing to back it up with your actions is like complimenting someone's cooking while quietly feeding it to the dog—it creates doubt and diminishes trust. True affirmation is as much about congruence as it is about words—your actions need to align with what you say, or your partner might start wondering if your compliments are just filled with hot air.

Actually, we have one more reason words of affirmation can get lost in translation: not knowing their dialect. That deserves a deep dive.

Discovering the Dialects of Affirmation

Just as every language has unique dialects, words of affirmation can take different forms depending on the individual. What feels meaningful and loving to one person might not resonate as deeply with another. To truly connect, it's important to go beyond general affirmations and understand the specific way your partner receives and interprets them. Discovering their dialect means paying attention to the words, tone, and delivery that matter most to them, ensuring your affirmations hit the mark every time.

There are three primary dialects of words of affirmation that help express love in ways tailored to your partner: **encouragement**, **appreciation**, and **compliments**.

Each serves a unique purpose—whether it's uplifting your partner during challenges, acknowledging their efforts or qualities, or simply making them feel seen and admired. By understanding which of these resonates most with your partner, you can speak their love language with greater clarity and impact.

WORDS OF AFFIRMATION DIALECT #1

Encouragement

It has been said that "our chief want is someone who will inspire us to be what we know we could be."[12] This is nowhere more evident than in a person with this dialect. Encouragement as a dialect of words of affirmation is about providing emotional support and confidence.

Is Encouragement Your Partner's Dialect?

Do they seem particularly uplifted or energized when you cheer them on or acknowledge their efforts? Do they talk about how much it means to have someone in their corner? If they frequently seek reassurance or share their fears and dreams with you, encouragement might be their go-to dialect. You know encouragement is your partner's dialect if:

- ☐ They light up when you acknowledge their efforts, even in small ways, and seem motivated to keep going.
- ☐ They often share their fears, uncertainties, or dreams with you, seeking your perspective or reassurance.
- ☐ They recall moments when someone's words of belief or support deeply impacted them.
- ☐ They frequently express appreciation for your encouragement, saying things like, "That means so much," or "I really needed to hear that."
- ☐ They feel particularly uplifted when you affirm their abilities or potential, especially during challenging times.
- ☐ They actively seek validation from you when they are unsure, asking, "Do you think I can do this?" or "What do you think about this idea?"
- ☐ They respond enthusiastically when you praise their courage, effort, or progress, even more than the results they achieve.

Would you say your partner checks a lot of these boxes? If so, they likely understand this dialect. And that means you're speaking their love language fluently whenever you're cheering them on when they feel uncertain. It's not about sugarcoating or false positivity but authentically recognizing their efforts and potential. Whether they're striving for a new achievement, recovering from a setback, or taking a leap of faith, encouragement communicates, "I believe in you."

Maya had been toying with the idea of launching a wellness blog.

She loved curating healthy recipes, sharing mindfulness tips, and writing about the little things that brought her joy. But deep down, she questioned whether anyone would care what she had to say.

One evening, she nervously floated the idea to her husband, Rob.

Without missing a beat, he said, "You'd be incredible at that. Seriously, Maya—you have a gift. People need your voice. Want me to help you brainstorm a name for the site?"

His words weren't just kind—they were catalytic.

That simple expression of belief lit something in Maya. It shifted her from self-doubt to forward motion. Within six months, her blog was live. A year later, she had a loyal following and partnerships she never imagined possible.

Encouragement wasn't just a nice gesture—it was the fuel Maya needed. It was Rob's way of speaking her love language. His words didn't flatter—they empowered. That's the heart of the encouragement dialect within words of affirmation: it sees potential and calls it forward.

Why Encouragement Matters

For some, encouragement is the most meaningful way to feel loved because it directly supports their growth, aspirations, and emotional well being. Life's challenges can make anyone feel overwhelmed or insecure, and hearing words of encouragement from a partner can be the difference between giving up and persevering. When you consistently provide encouragement, you're not just affirming their value—you're showing that you're invested in their journey and rooting for their success.

Encouragement also strengthens trust and emotional connection in a relationship. When your partner knows you believe in them, they're more likely to share their dreams, struggles, and vulnerabilities with you. It creates a safe space where they feel supported, even in their weakest moments.

WORDS OF AFFIRMATION DIALECT #2

Appreciation

The dialect of appreciation in words of affirmation focuses on recognizing and valuing the unique contributions your partner brings to the relationship and the world around them. It's not just about thanking them for what they do—it's about truly seeing and acknowledging who they are. For someone who resonates with this dialect, expressions of gratitude and admiration fill their emotional tank, reinforcing that their efforts and qualities are noticed and cherished. Whether it's appreciating a small act of kindness or highlighting a deeper personal trait, this kind of affirmation makes them feel seen, valued, and loved.

Is Appreciation Your Partner's Dialect?

Does your partner light up when you express gratitude for them? Do they seem especially moved when you acknowledge their thoughtfulness, hard work, or unique qualities? If expressions of thanks or admiration make them feel deeply seen and valued, appreciation might be their primary dialect. You know appreciation is your partner's dialect if:

- ☐ They beam with pride when you thank them for small acts of kindness or effort, even the ones they don't expect recognition for.
- ☐ They often express how much it means when someone notices their contributions or says "Thank you."
- ☐ They are quick to show gratitude themselves and may model the behavior they most crave.
- ☐ They respond enthusiastically when you highlight qualities or traits you admire, such as their compassion, creativity, or dependability.

- ☐ They feel especially connected to you when you make an effort to recognize their contributions publicly or privately.
- ☐ They seem energized by acknowledgments of who they are, not just what they do, such as, "You have such a gift for making people feel at ease."
- ☐ They often recall moments when someone's gratitude or admiration made a lasting impression on them.

If this sounds like your partner, it's a strong indication that the dialect of appreciation resonates with them. By noticing and articulating what you admire about their character, efforts, or contributions, you're filling their emotional tank in a way that feels personal and meaningful. This isn't about empty praise—it's about truly seeing and valuing who they are and the unique role they play in your life.

Bill didn't grow up hearing "Thank you." His dad drank too much. His mom struggled with depression.

So even though he was the one doing the dishes every night and washing the car every Saturday, no one ever acknowledged it. The silence taught him to expect nothing for his effort—just do the job and move on.

By his early twenties, Bill had married Madeline. They both worked demanding jobs, but they genuinely enjoyed building a life together. After dinner—usually made by Madeline—Bill would clear the plates and start on the dishes. On Saturdays he was out front giving the car a fresh shine. Not because he expected anything in return.

But Madeline noticed. And she *said* something.

"Thanks for doing the dishes, babe. That really helps me breathe after a long day." "I love that you take such good care of the car. It makes me feel proud when we pull into the driveway."

At first, Bill didn't know how to respond. It felt unfamiliar. But good. Like something he didn't know he needed.

Soon, he found himself asking, "Anything else I can do today to make your life a little easier?"

That's the power of appreciation as a dialect within words of affirmation. It doesn't just say "I love you." It says, "I see you. What you do matters." For someone like Bill, who grew up without those words, it was like water to dry ground. His love tank was full—and overflowing.

Why Appreciation Matters

Feeling appreciated is one of the deepest ways to feel loved and valued. In the busyness of daily life, it's easy for contributions—big or small—to go unnoticed. But when you take the time to acknowledge your partner's efforts, character, or thoughtfulness, it sends a powerful message: *I see you, and you matter.*

Appreciation has a unique way of building trust and fostering emotional intimacy. When your partner knows that what they do is noticed and valued, it deepens their sense of connection and belonging in the relationship. It's not just about saying "Thank you" for the obvious things, it's about noticing the details that make them who they are and expressing gratitude for those qualities.

Whether it's acknowledging their kindness, recognizing their sacrifices, or simply appreciating their presence, words within this dialect communicate love in a way that helps your partner feel truly seen and cherished.

WORDS OF AFFIRMATION DIALECT #3

Compliments

The dialect of compliments within words of affirmation is all about admiration and expressing love through uplifting remarks about your partner's appearance, personality, or achievements. It's not just flattery—it's about offering genuine, thoughtful statements that make your partner feel special. For someone who resonates with this dialect, a well-timed compliment can brighten their day and reinforce their sense of worth.

Compliments focus on celebrating your partner, whether it's a quick remark about how amazing they look today or a heartfelt acknowledgment of a quality you admire, like their sense of humor or determination. This kind of affirmation communicates admiration and attention, letting them know you're noticing the little things that make them unique. For those who value this dialect, compliments don't just boost confidence—they make them feel adored, cherished, and deeply appreciated.

Are Compliments Your Partner's Dialect?

Does your partner's mood noticeably lift when you acknowledge their appearance, praise their accomplishments, or point out qualities you admire? Do they seem especially energized when you notice their unique qualities or express your admiration? If compliments make your partner feel seen, valued, and adored, this may be their primary dialect. You know compliments are your partner's dialect if:

- ☐ They light up when you praise their appearance, like a new haircut or outfit.
- ☐ They seem deeply moved when you recognize and vocalize a specific quality you admire, such as their humor, kindness, or creativity.
- ☐ They often replay compliments in their mind or mention how much a specific remark meant to them.
- ☐ They enjoy receiving compliments in private but may feel especially appreciated when you express admiration in public settings.

- ☐ They seem particularly confident and uplifted after you acknowledge their efforts, talents, or accomplishments.
- ☐ They frequently comment on how much compliments mean to them or how they remember kind words from the past.
- ☐ They actively seek feedback, asking questions like, "Do you think I did a good job?" or "How does this look?"

If this list resonates with your partner, it's a strong sign that compliments are how they feel most loved. Thoughtful and genuine compliments communicate that you're paying attention to the things that make them special. This isn't about shallow flattery—it's about offering meaningful words that reinforce their value and show your admiration for who they are.

Julie had a gift—and Richard knew it.

She was a pro at giving compliments, and not the generic kind.

After a rough day, she'd look at him and say, "Your sense of humor is one of my favorite things about you. You always know how to help me shake off the stress."

Or while he was flipping burgers on the grill, she'd lean in and say, "You know, I don't take it lightly that you cook dinner twice a week. That's not just helpful—it's sexy. You're seriously the best husband ever."

Richard would usually chuckle and say something like, "Okay, okay, don't oversell it."

But inside? He was glowing.

Those words weren't fluff. They landed. They built him up.

Compliments were Richard's dialect. And Julie? She spoke it with fluency, precision, and heart.

For someone like Richard, a well-placed compliment wasn't just nice to hear—it was love, out loud.

Why Compliments Matter

Compliments have a way of cutting through the noise of daily life, offering your partner a moment of pure affirmation. For someone who thrives on this dialect, a thoughtful compliment can feel like being seen in the best possible light. It's not about saying something just to say it—it's about reflecting back to your partner the qualities, traits, or efforts that make them lovable. A genuine compliment doesn't just boost their confidence, it reminds them how connected they are to you.

Compliments also nurture a sense of admiration and appreciation in the relationship. When you take the time to notice and celebrate your partner's qualities—whether it's their sense of humor, their determination, or even how good they look in what they're wearing—it reinforces their value to you. For someone who values this dialect, these words aren't trivial, they are affirmations of love and affection that speak directly to their heart.

When it comes to words of affirmation, we've unpacked the three most common dialects of this love language: encouragement, appreciation, and compliments. Each one has its own flavor—whether it's cheering your partner on, noticing and valuing what they do, or simply telling them how great they are. Sure, there may be other ways to express this love language, but these three cover the heart of what matters most. The key is figuring out which one speaks loudest to your partner so your words hit home in the best possible way.

Speaking of that, affirming your partner is definitely a good thing, but too much of a good thing can sometimes backfire.

Avoiding Affirmation Overload

While words of affirmation are essential for someone who values this love language, it's absolutely possible to overdo it. Too much affirmation—especially if it feels like you're handing out participation trophies—can dilute its impact and even create skepticism. If every time they empty the dishwasher you're declaring, "You're the most amazing human to ever walk this earth," your partner might start wondering if your words are heartfelt or if you've just switched to autopilot. Meaningful affirmations should feel thoughtful, not like something you're required to say because there's a quota to fill.

To avoid affirmation overload, focus on quality over quantity. Instead of tossing out generic compliments like, "You're awesome," take the time to notice specific things your partner does or qualities that truly stand out. Highlighting something meaningful—like their patience with a tough situation or how they brighten someone's day with their humor—has way more impact than a nonstop stream of surface-level praise. By reserving affirmations for the moments that genuinely matter, you'll ensure your words hit home and don't start sounding like a motivational poster.

Remember Mary Jackson's story at the beginning of our chapter? It reminds us that the right words, spoken at the right time, can inspire courage, validate worth, and even transform a life. But just as language is nuanced, so too is the way we express words of affirmation.

Understanding your partner's unique dialect is key to ensuring your words land with the impact you intend. While one dialect—encouragement, appreciation, or compliments—often resonates most deeply, people with this love language often connect with more than one. Learning to discern which dialect speaks most profoundly in the moment is valuable, but you'll rarely go wrong with any of these expressions if your partner thrives on affirming words.

Someone once said, "Kind words can be short and easy to speak, but their echoes are truly endless."[13] So, choose your words thoughtfully—because the love they carry can last a lifetime.

TAKE THE NEXT STEP

Uncovering your partner's specific dialect of words of affirmation can transform how you express love through language. **The 5 Love Languages Premium Assessment** helps you pinpoint exactly how your partner receives affirmations best, offering personalized insights into the words, tone, and expressions that mean the most to them. It's a powerful tool to ensure your affirmations are not just heard—but truly felt.

Take the Premium Assessment today and discover how to speak words of affirmation in a way that strengthens your connection and builds your partner up.

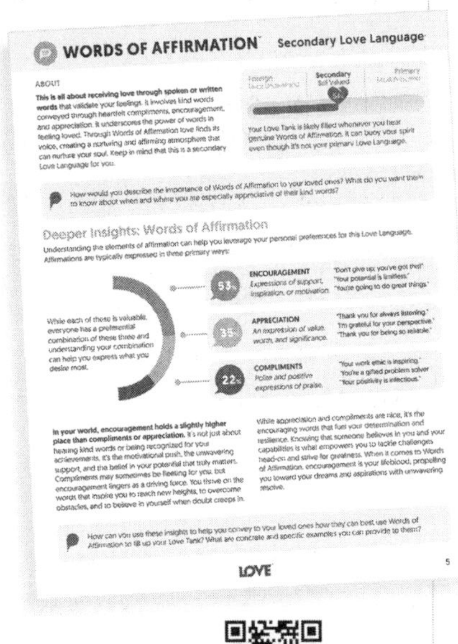

WORDS OF AFFIRMATION Secondary Love Language

ABOUT

This is all about receiving love through spoken or written words that validate your feelings. It involves kind words conveyed through heartfelt compliments, encouragement, and appreciation. It underscores the power of words in feeling loved. Through Words of Affirmation love finds its voice, creating a nurturing and affirming atmosphere that can nurture your soul. Keep in mind that this is a secondary Love Language for you.

Secondary
Still Valued

Your Love Tank is likely filled whenever you hear genuine Words of Affirmation. It can buoy your spirit even though it's not your primary Love Language.

How would you describe the importance of Words of Affirmation to your loved ones? What do you want them to know about when and where you are especially appreciative of their kind words?

Deeper Insights: Words of Affirmation

Understanding the elements of affirmation can help you leverage your personal preferences for this Love Language. Affirmations are typically expressed in three primary ways:

While each of these is valuable, everyone has a preferential combination of these three and understanding your combination can help you express what you desire most.

53% **ENCOURAGEMENT** Expressions of support, inspiration, or motivation. "Don't give up; you've got this!" "Your potential is limitless." "You're going to do great things."

APPRECIATION *An expression of value, worth, and significance.* "Thank you for always listening." "I'm grateful for your perspective." "Thank you for being so reliable."

22% **COMPLIMENTS** *Polite and positive expressions of praise.* "Your work ethic is inspiring." "You're a gifted problem solver." "Your positivity is infectious."

In your world, encouragement holds a slightly higher place than compliments or appreciation. It's not just about hearing kind words or being recognized for your achievements, it's the motivational push, the unwavering support, and the belief in your potential that truly matters. Compliments may sometimes be fleeting for you, but encouragement lingers as a driving force. You thrive on the words that inspire you to reach new heights, to overcome obstacles, and to believe in yourself when doubt creeps in.

While appreciation and compliments are nice, it's the encouraging words that fuel your determination and resilience. Knowing that someone believes in you and your capabilities is what empowers you to tackle challenges head-on and strive for greatness. When it comes to Words of Affirmation, encouragement is your lifeblood, propelling you toward your dreams and aspirations with unwavering resolve.

How can you use these insights to help you convey to your loved ones how they can best use Words of Affirmation to fill up your Love Tank? What are concrete and specific examples you can provide to them?

LOVE

5

5LoveLanguages.com/Premium

CHAPTER 8

Quality Time

Creating Moments That Truly Matter

In 1973, as America wrestled with the turbulence of Watergate, the Vietnam War's aftermath, and a growing oil crisis, music became a vital escape—a way to find comfort amid the chaos. During this time, a tender song by singer-songwriter Jim Croce seemed to echo everywhere, offering a poignant reminder of what truly matters.

"Time in a Bottle" became the number one hit that autumn, its soft melody and heartfelt lyrics resonating with listeners across the country. The song revealed Croce's poignant longing to "save every day till eternity passes" just to spend them with the one he loved. Its haunting chorus struck a universal chord, lamenting how "there never seems to be enough time" with those we hold dear.

Tragically, the song's personal significance deepened just days after its release. On September 20, 1973, Jim Croce boarded a small aircraft in Natchitoches, Louisiana. As the plane attempted to take off from a dimly lit airstrip, it clipped a treetop at the runway's edge, crashing and killing Croce along with five others on board.

His wife, Ingrid Croce, was left to raise their infant son alone, grappling with the devastating loss of her husband. For Ingrid, "Time in a Bottle" must have become a bittersweet anthem, echoing through every corner of her life.

She once shared how the song—and the painful reality it represented—shaped her perspective. In Croce's, the restaurant Ingrid owned in San Diego, a mural of Jim graced the back wall, which served as an inspiration to her about remembering how fragile life is and to never take for granted the time we have with the ones we love.

Croce's music often reflected on our human desire to reach back and grasp moments already gone. Songs like "Operator" and "I've Got a Name" captured the ache of time slipping through our fingers. In his brief thirty years, Jim Croce seemed to understand what so many of us only come to realize too late: the fleeting nature of life and the sacredness of time shared with those we love.

And chances are, you feel this too. Time moves faster than we'd like, slipping away even as we long to hold on to it. If we could save time in a bottle, we all know what we'd want to do with it. Yet too often, the time we have—those precious hours given to us each day—is carelessly squandered. The challenge isn't just finding time but making time, intentionally, for the person that matters most.

We all feel it, but people with quality time as their primary love language feel it even more deeply. For them, time isn't just a commodity to be managed—it's a treasure to be shared. It's not about what you're doing, but that you're doing it together, fully present and engaged. For this person, moments of undivided attention, where distractions are set aside, communicate love in ways that words or actions alone can't.

This chapter is about understanding how to make time matter. It's about discovering how intentional moments—whether they're as simple as a walk around the block or as planned as a weekend getaway—can create lasting connections. Because for someone whose love language is quality time, there's no better way to say "I love you" than by giving the one thing you can't get back: your time.

A Quick Review

Quality time is about undivided attention and shared experiences (see chapter 5 in *The 5 Love Languages* for an overview). It's not just being in the same space—it's being fully present. For someone whose heart resonates with this love language, meaningful connection through time spent together is essential to feeling valued and loved.

Ways to Practice **Quality Time**

- *Turning off your phone and having an uninterrupted conversation over coffee.*
- *Taking a walk together and asking thoughtful questions about their day (with plenty of follow-up questions).*
- *Planning a date night around something they love, like a movie marathon or a visit to their favorite museum.*
- *Working on a shared hobby or project, like cooking, gardening, playing a board game, or doing a puzzle.*
- *Taking a day trip to explore a nearby town or park, creating shared adventures and memories.*

For those who thrive on quality time, it's generally not about how much time you spend—it's about the quality of that time. Intentional focus and genuine connection matter most to them.

As we explore this love language further, you'll discover how to tailor your time together to reflect your partner's unique preferences, turning ordinary moments into lasting memories.

Why Quality Time Speaks Straight to the Heart

Spending time together is, of course, valuable in any relationship. But for some, it's the fastest way to their heart. They love focused, undistracted attention. It's their ultimate expression of love. Early experiences often shape this love language—growing up in environments where time together was either prioritized or neglected influences how we associate presence with love and belonging. Whether bridging a gap or deepening a bond, quality time creates moments of closeness that feel deeply meaningful.

Those drawn to this love language are highly attuned to presence and engagement. For those who experienced distance or inconsistency in relationships growing up, intentional time together can heal wounds and restore trust. For those with secure attachments, shared time serves as a relational superglue, strengthening the sense of connection and stability.

On a relational level, quality time fosters emotional intimacy. It's not about the activity but the attention given during it. Whether it's a deep conversation, a shared hobby, or simply being together in the same space and listening to music, these moments communicate, "You matter to me, and I'm here with you."

Personality traits also play their role. Reflective and emotionally expressive individuals may value deep, uninterrupted conversations, while adventurous or curious types may cherish shared activities and experiences. Regardless of personality, the core need remains the same: undivided attention that nurtures connection.

For someone who thrives on quality time, it's not about the quantity of hours—it's about the intentionality and presence shared in those moments. Whether through grand adventures or quiet evenings, spending meaningful time together is their strongest proof of love, speaking straight to their heart in a way nothing else can.

When Quality Time Matters Most

Quality time is always meaningful, but there are moments in a relationship when it becomes absolutely essential. These are the times when shared presence isn't just appreciated—it's transformative.

Times of Loneliness

For someone whose primary love language is quality time, moments of loneliness or isolation hit especially hard. These are times when they may feel disconnected or overlooked—not just in the relationship but in life overall. Loneliness might stem from external circumstances like a lack of close friendships, loss of a loved one, professional struggles, or even the emotional toll of life transitions. In these moments, they long for the steady, grounding presence of their partner to remind them they are not alone.

Your focused attention during these times can be a lifeline. For example, dedicating an afternoon to be fully present—no phones, no distractions—can communicate, "You matter to me, and I want to be with you."

Failing to offer your presence during these vulnerable moments may deepen their sense of isolation. However, showing up fully can renew their sense of security, not only in the relationship but in themselves.

Times of Anticipation

Moments of shared excitement—planning a big event, preparing for a trip, or simply looking forward to a special occasion—are when quality time shines. For someone who values shared experiences, anticipation is an opportunity to connect deeply through planning and dreaming together.

Quality time during these moments builds connection not just in the present but in the promise of a shared future. When you join in their excitement and match their energy, you're communicating that you don't just love them—you love experiencing life with them.

Times of Emotional Drift

Relationships naturally ebb and flow, and times of emotional drift—when life gets busy, stress builds, or routines become a rut—are particularly important for someone who values quality time. These are moments when the relationship might feel distant, not because of conflict, but because connection has slipped through the cracks.

Making time to reconnect through intentional activities, like setting aside a weekly date night or creating space for uninterrupted conversation, can reignite the bond. Even something as simple as turning off the TV and sharing a meal at the table can restore a sense of closeness.

When Not to Focus on Quality Time

While quality time is deeply meaningful, there are moments when prioritizing it can feel forced, misplaced, or even counterproductive. Recognizing when to step back is as crucial as knowing when to lean in. Quality time should always feel organic even though it's intentional—pushing for it at the wrong moment can undermine its value.

For example, avoid pressing for togetherness when your partner clearly needs space. If they're processing stress or overwhelmed by a situation, suggesting, "Let's just spend some time together, it'll help," might feel out of touch. Or if your partner is engaged in something they're passionate about—like a work project or time with friends—pushing for quality time can feel intrusive. Respecting their independence and allowing them to fully enjoy those moments without interruption shows care and trust.

Another time to tread carefully is during moments of conflict. If quality time is proposed as a way to avoid addressing a problem—"Let's just watch a movie and forget about it"—it can come across as an attempt to sidestep meaningful resolution. Quality time should enhance connection, not be used as a form of denial or distraction from important issues.

For those who value this love language, the timing and context of shared moments matter. Insisting on quality time when it's not welcome or appropriate risks turning a source of connection into a point of tension. Knowing when to wait ensures that your time together will be truly meaningful when the moment is right.

How Quality Time Can Get Lost in Translation

So you know your partner's love language is quality time. You're all in. Your heart is in the right place. You've read and reread the chapter in *The 5 Love Languages*. But your efforts aren't quite landing the way you'd like. What's going on?

It may have to do with emphasizing proximity over presence. Simply watching TV together might feel like quality time to you, but for your partner? Maybe not. It may lack the depth or engagement they crave. For someone who values this love language, it's not just about being near each other—it's about actively connecting.

Another way quality time can miss the mark is when it feels forced. For example, suggesting, "Let's spend time together now because I'm going to be busy later," is likely to come across as more about checking a box than genuinely wanting to connect. Your partner may feel pressured rather than appreciated.

Timing is everything. Trying to engage in quality time when your partner is distracted or stressed—like suggesting a long conversation when they're in the middle of a busy workday—can leave them feeling overwhelmed or frustrated. Instead, consider their current state and offer an activity that aligns with what they need, such as a short walk to help them decompress.

Finally, quality time can lose its impact when paired with distractions. True quality time means giving your full attention, ensuring they feel valued and prioritized.

Actually, there's one more reason quality time can miss the mark: not knowing your partner's preferences for how they like to spend time together. That deserves its own discussion.

Discovering the Dialects of Quality Time

Quality time, like any love language, has its own distinct dialects—different ways of expressing and experiencing time together. For those who value this love language, the way time is spent matters just as much as the time itself. Not all shared moments hold the same weight, and what feels meaningful to one person might not resonate with another. To truly connect, it's essential to understand the specific ways your partner experiences love through time spent together.

There are four primary dialects of quality time: **improvising**, **managing**, **planning**, and **dreaming**. Each reflects a unique approach to sharing time, and they are formed from various combinations of being scheduled vs. unscheduled, and present oriented vs. future oriented. The diagram on the right sheds some light.

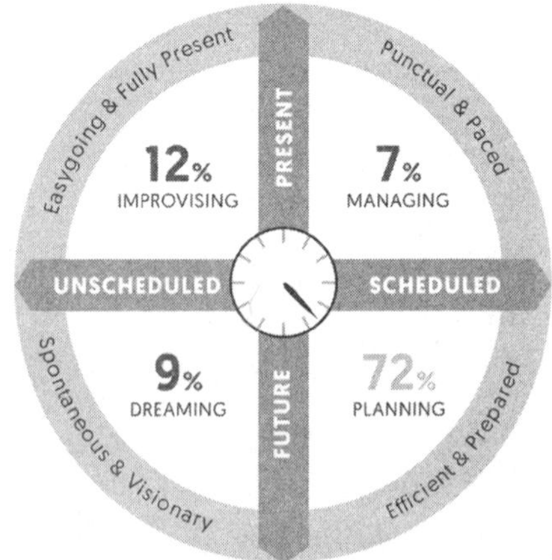

By learning which of these speaks most clearly to your partner, you can ensure that the time you spend together feels intentional, fulfilling, and deeply connected.

In the sections ahead, we'll unpack these four dialects, exploring how each one can help you make the most of your time together and create lasting memories with the person you love.

QUALITY TIME DIALECT #1

Improvising

Improvising as a dialect of quality time is all about spontaneity and being fully present in the moment. It's not driven by calendars or to-do lists but by the simple joy of spending time together, wherever the day might take you. This dialect thrives on being unscheduled and embracing the here and now. Whether it's taking an unplanned detour to watch the sunset or deciding to turn a rainy afternoon into a board game marathon, improvising celebrates the beauty of shared experiences that unfold naturally—without being dictated by schedules.

As writer E. B. White once said, "I arise in the morning torn between a desire to improve (or save) the world and a desire to enjoy (or savor) the world."[14] For those who value this dialect, quality time isn't about perfect plans—it's about enjoying life's unexpected moments together, creating memories that feel effortless and unforced.

Is Improvising Your Partner's Dialect?

Does your partner seem most energized when plans are unstructured and free-flowing? Do they thrive on spur-of-the-moment ideas, like suggesting a spontaneous picnic or taking an unplanned walk through the neighborhood? If the joy of simply being together in the moment resonates most with your partner, improvising may be their primary quality time dialect.

You know improvising is your partner's dialect if:

- ☐ They seem happiest when your time together is unscheduled, allowing the moment to unfold naturally.
- ☐ They light up when you suggest an impromptu activity, like grabbing coffee or watching the sunset without planning ahead.
- ☐ They get excited by unexpected detours during the day, like stopping at a roadside stand or trying out a new spot on a whim.
- ☐ They value presence over planning, focusing on being fully engaged with you rather than sticking to a fixed agenda.
- ☐ They rarely suggest concrete plans ahead of time but show enthusiasm for whatever feels right in the moment.
- ☐ They often express frustration with rigid schedules, preferring flexibility in how you spend time together.
- ☐ They see unplanned moments as opportunities for creativity and connection, often saying things like, "Let's just see where the day takes us."

If this list resonates with your partner, improvising is likely how they feel most loved. For someone with this dialect, the magic of quality time isn't in elaborate plans but in the serendipity of shared, unscripted moments. By embracing spontaneity and staying present, you'll speak this dialect fluently and make your partner feel truly seen and valued.

You may not be a spur-of-the-moment person. Unplanned activities can feel like interruptions, not invitations. But if your partner's love language is quality time and their dialect is improvising, you may have a learning curve. The good news? With love as your motivation—"I want to fill their love tank and keep it full"—you *can* learn to speak their dialect.

That was Sarah's story. Spontaneity didn't come naturally to her. She liked schedules, checklists, and knowing what came next. But she knew Todd thrived on shared moments that weren't scripted—last-minute drives, unexpected coffee dates, random detours just to chase a sunset.

So she got intentional. She wrote a sticky note and placed it in her Bible—the one she read each morning. It said: "Todd's dialect is improvising. Today, I'll welcome one interruption to show him love."

Each day, she prayed for grace to embrace the unexpected. At first, it felt awkward and disruptive. But within a few months, something shifted. She wasn't just tolerating the spontaneity—she was starting to enjoy it.

What began as unnatural became a new rhythm.

For Sarah, it was like learning a new language. But the more she practiced, the more fluent she became. And with every impromptu moment she leaned into, she wasn't just speaking Todd's dialect—she was speaking love.

Why Improvising Matters

Improvising matters because it captures the beauty of living in the moment. For those who connect with this dialect, the spontaneity and freedom of unscheduled time together communicate love in its most relaxed and authentic form.

When you embrace improvising with your partner, you show them that they're not just part of your schedule—they're part of your life in real time. The unplanned nature of improvising brings an element of surprise and excitement to your time together, fostering creativity and connection. It keeps your relationship fresh and dynamic.

Improvising also removes the pressure of perfection, reminding both of you that the most meaningful moments don't require planning or preparation—they just need presence. Unscripted presence.

QUALITY TIME DIALECT #2

Managing

Managing as a dialect of quality time thrives on structure and reliability. For those who connect with this dialect, shared time is most meaningful when it's planned, punctual, and runs at a steady, predictable pace. It's not about rigid schedules, but rather about honoring the commitment to be present together at the agreed-upon time and giving that moment your full attention.

Whether it's a regular weekly date night, a morning coffee routine, or simply sticking to a plan without distractions, managing emphasizes the value of creating intentional rhythms. For this dialect, time shared isn't just about the present—it's about respecting it, making the most of what's promised, and showing your partner they can rely on you.

Is Managing Your Partner's Dialect?

Does your partner seem most at ease when your shared time is predictable and runs smoothly? Do they thrive on planned-for, structured moments where your focus is entirely on each other? If they value consistency and reliability in how you spend time together, managing may be their primary quality time dialect.

You know managing is your partner's dialect if:

- ☐ They appreciate punctuality and seem unsettled when plans run late or feel chaotic.
- ☐ They find comfort in predictable rhythms, like watching a favorite show together every evening or sharing a daily morning coffee.
- ☐ They value having a clear plan for your time together and express frustration when things feel disorganized or last minute.

- ☐ They thrive on knowing you'll prioritize them by reserving uninterrupted time just for the two of you.
- ☐ They feel reassured when plans go off without a hitch, often commenting on how much they appreciate that things went smoothly.
- ☐ They light up when you make plans in advance and stick to them, such as setting a regular date night or weekend routine.
- ☐ They love when your actions show dependability, such as honoring commitments to spend time together even on busy days.

Managing is likely their dialect if this list resonates with your partner. For someone with this dialect, shared time isn't just about being together—it's about creating a reliable and structured space where they feel secure and valued. By being intentional, punctual, and present, you can connect deeply with a partner who values managing.

A few months into marriage, Chloe started to feel something she hadn't expected: distance.

She and Zack both worked full-time, and several nights a week, Zack brought work home. It wasn't like he was ignoring her—he just had deadlines. But Chloe kept thinking, *We had more time together when we were dating than we do now.*

One night, she brought it up.

Zack shrugged and said, "It's just reality. Life is busy."

To him, it was logical. But to Chloe, it felt dismissive. She didn't need hours—she needed *intentionality.*

Then she attended a marriage conference where she heard a simple idea: daily sharing time. Each evening, couples set aside a few minutes to name three things that happened in their day and how they felt about them. The examples were small—"I stopped for gas." "How did you feel?" "Annoyed. Prices are ridiculous."

That idea clicked for Chloe.

She wasn't craving grand gestures—she was craving scheduled presence. Connection with a place on the calendar. So she pitched it to Zack, and to her surprise, he agreed to try.

They picked a consistent time—right after dinner. No phones, no multitasking. Just ten minutes of eye contact and undivided attention.

Within two weeks, Chloe felt a shift.

She didn't have to chase connection anymore. It was showing up, on time, every night. Her love tank started to refill. And with that renewed emotional closeness, their weekends naturally grew more fun and connected too.

Zack had always cared. He just hadn't known how to speak her dialect—until now.

For Chloe, love meant being seen, heard, and scheduled in. That's the managing dialect within quality time: consistent, present-oriented connection that happens *on purpose*.

Why Managing Matters

Managing matters because it creates a sense of stability and reliability in your shared time. For those who resonate with this dialect, the predictability and structure of well-managed moments communicate respect and intentionality.

When you manage your time together, it reassures your partner that they are a priority, not an afterthought. For this person, thoughtful management fosters trust and deepens connection, creating a foundation where love can thrive.

Managing also helps eliminate the chaos and stress that can disrupt quality time. It brings a steady rhythm to your relationship, making your time together feel effortless and enjoyable. For someone who values this dialect, managing isn't about rigid schedules or being in a rut—it's about building a space where connection feels secure, thoughtful, and intentional.

QUALITY TIME DIALECT #3

Planning

Planning as a dialect of quality time is all about looking ahead with intention and preparation. For those who resonate with this dialect, meaningful time together often begins with a well-thought-out plan. They thrive on efficiency and love creating shared experiences that are carefully crafted to make the most of the future.

Whether it's booking tickets for an upcoming event, mapping out a dream vacation, or even just coordinating the week's date nights in advance, planning reflects the value of investing effort into creating purposeful moments. This dialect speaks to the joy of anticipation and the assurance that time spent together is prioritized and thoughtfully arranged.

Is Planning Your Partner's Dialect?

Does your partner light up when time together is carefully thought out and purposeful? Do they thrive on well-crafted plans that make the most of your shared time? If they love the anticipation of what's ahead and value the effort you put into creating memorable experiences, planning may be their primary quality time dialect.

You know planning is your partner's dialect if:

- ☐ They appreciate when you map out time together, whether it's a weekend getaway, a dinner reservation, or even just planning the week ahead.
- ☐ They get excited about upcoming events or activities that have been intentionally prepared.
- ☐ They seem energized by the idea of maximizing your time together and value efficiency in how it's spent.
- ☐ They thrive on knowing the details are handled, such as booking tickets, making reservations, or coordinating schedules.

- ☐ They feel cared for when you proactively think ahead and create moments that show effort and thoughtfulness.
- ☐ They find joy in the process of preparing together, such as brainstorming ideas for future plans or collaborating on special events.
- ☐ They often express frustration when time is wasted due to a lack of preparation or last-minute decision-making.

If the majority of this list resonates with your partner, planning is likely how they feel most loved. For someone with this dialect, the act of preparing for time together—whether it's a small moment or a grand adventure—is a tangible expression of care and commitment. By being proactive and intentional, you can create meaningful experiences that deeply resonate with a partner who values planning.

Josh and Lilly shared the same love language *and* the same dialect—an uncommon match. Both were planners. They had a standing date night each week, alternating who chose the restaurant. They loved trying new places. Every summer, they planned their vacation together—he picked the destination one year, she the next. Reservations were always made months in advance. Their love tanks were full, and life felt beautifully in sync.

Most couples aren't so aligned. When one is a planner and the other an improviser, conflict is likely. But conflict can also be an opportunity for growth. It starts with listening—truly understanding each other's perspective. You're different, but you're on the same team.

One simple strategy: Agree that once a month, the planner chooses and organizes something for the two of you. The improviser joins in as an act of love. Then the improviser picks a spontaneous idea for the day, and the planner embraces it as a loving gesture.

Both are choosing to love in the way that speaks most deeply to the other—and that's the key to a thriving marriage.

Why Planning Matters

"Failing to plan is planning to fail." The person with this dialect takes this maxim to heart. Planning is a big part of their love language because it transforms intention into action. For those who connect with this dialect, the thought and effort that go into planning signal care, and commitment.

When you plan with your partner, it brings them joy. Whether it's a thoughtfully planned date night or mapping out the next decade, planning demonstrates consideration and a desire to make the most of your shared time.

Planning also creates anticipation and excitement, giving your partner something to look forward to. It offers a sense of security and stability, knowing your time together is valued enough to be intentionally set apart. For someone who values this dialect, planning isn't just preparation—it's an act of love that turns ordinary time into extraordinary moments.

QUALITY TIME DIALECT #4

Dreaming

Looking toward the future with excitement and imagination. That's what the dreaming dialect of quality time is all about. For those who connect with this dialect, meaningful time together often involves spontaneous, visionary conversations about what's to come. It's not about rigid plans or detailed schedules—it's about letting your imagination take the lead as you envision possibilities together.

Whether it's dreaming up future vacations, brainstorming life goals, or imagining the house you'll build one day, this dialect thrives on creativity and connection. They love dreaming together about possibilities.

Dreaming creates a sense of shared purpose and fuels hope for the future, reminding both partners that the best days are still ahead—and they'll enjoy them together.

Is Dreaming Your Partner's Dialect?

Does your partner come alive when conversations drift toward the future—brainstorming goals, imagining possibilities, and sharing visions of what could be? Do they seem most connected when the two of you are dreaming together, letting your imagination run free? If they value open-ended, visionary conversations over more detailed plans, dreaming may be their primary quality time dialect.

You know dreaming is your partner's dialect if:

- ☐ They love talking about future plans in broad strokes, such as envisioning vacations, life goals, or creative ideas.
- ☐ They seem energized by spontaneous "what if" conversations that spark imagination and hope.
- ☐ They find joy in sharing their dreams with you and feel deeply connected when you show interest in their vision for the future.
- ☐ They prefer flexibility over rigid planning, enjoying the freedom to explore possibilities without locking anything down.
- ☐ They value the connection that comes from dreaming out loud, rather than focusing solely on execution.
- ☐ They often start conversations with phrases like, "Wouldn't it be great if . . . ?" or "Imagine if we could . . ."
- ☐ They light up when you join in their enthusiasm, building on their ideas and creating a shared sense of excitement about the future.

Would your partner check most of these boxes? If so, dreaming is likely how they feel most loved. For someone with this dialect, quality time is about sharing a vision for what's ahead and finding joy in the possibilities together. By engaging their imagination and joining in their future-focused conversations, you create a connection that inspires hope and deepens your bond.

Dreams don't always match reality. They may come true—or they may not. But dreamers still love to dream. And more than anything, they want their partner to join them in those dreams. That's when they feel most loved.

Nathan was married to a dreamer. His wife, Sandy, often started conversations with "What if . . .?" Before reading *The 5 Love Languages*, Nathan dismissed her as unrealistic—and told her so. Sandy felt shut down and unloved.

But after taking the Premium Assessment, Nathan discovered Sandy's love language was quality time, and her dialect was dreaming. That insight changed everything.

Nathan began listening—not just patiently, but with curiosity. He asked questions, let her expand her thoughts, and even shared ideas of his own. He still knew some dreams might never come true—but now, that wasn't the point. Loving her meant dreaming with her.

Their relationship warmed, and Sandy felt accepted and deeply loved. And who knows? When two people dream together, amazing things can happen.

Why Dreaming Matters

This dialect fuels hope, imagination, and connection. It matters because the act of envisioning the future together creates a deep sense of shared purpose. Exploring possibilities and dreaming out loud with someone who truly listens and values your vision underscores a shared future.

When you engage in dreaming with your partner, you're not just talking about the future—you're building a bridge to it. Dreaming fosters emotional intimacy by creating a shared space where aspirations and ideas can grow freely. It shows your partner that you care about their hopes and dreams, and that you're invested in creating a future together.

In a world that often demands practicality and immediate results, dreaming offers the gift of possibility. It reminds your partner that life is more than schedules and to-do lists—it's a canvas waiting to be painted with your collective ideas. Dreaming isn't just idle conversation; it's an act of love that strengthens your connection and keeps your relationship forward-looking and inspired.

When it comes to quality time, we've explored the four most meaningful dialects of this love language: improvising, managing, planning, and dreaming. These four dialects capture the heart of what matters most to the person who treasures quality time. And, of course, your partner may value all of them at different times, but they're likely to have one that dominates.

But like all of the love languages, it's possible to overdo it and create a quality time overload.

Avoiding Quality Time Overload

When couples are dating, it's pretty normal to want to spend every waking moment together—because everything feels new and exciting, and who wouldn't want to hang out with their favorite person 24/7? But as time goes on, that level of nonstop togetherness can start to feel less like a romantic montage and more like being glued at the hip with no escape hatch. Even for someone who values quality time, it's not about spending *all* your time together—it's about making the time you do share feel meaningful.

To avoid quality time overload, remember that quality beats quantity every time. Watching hours of Netflix together without saying a word might technically count as "time," but it doesn't necessarily count as "quality." Instead, plan an intentional date or have a real conversation—bonus points if it doesn't involve your phones.

It's also important to give each other room to breathe. If your partner starts looking longingly at their headphones or escaping to "run errands" a little too often, it might be time to pull back. By balancing intentional togetherness with individual space, you ensure that the time you do spend together feels refreshing, fun, and something they actually look forward to. After all, absence makes the heart grow fonder . . . and gives you something to talk about when you're back together.

"There never seems to be enough time to do the things you want to do once you find them." When Jim Croce penned that sentence, he was speaking to the heart of all of us, but especially the person who is hardwired for quality time. They long for moments of connection that make life and love meaningful.

And here's the beautiful thing about time—it's not about how much you have, but how you use what you have. Even brief, intentional moments can create the kind of memories that last a lifetime. All we have to do is show up. Fully.

As Croce's song reminds us, we can't literally "save time in a bottle." But we can cherish the time we have by making it count. For someone who values quality time, these shared experiences aren't just a part of life—they are the heartbeat of love. So don't wait. Take the time, be present, and create the kind of moments that will matter long after the minutes have passed.

TAKE THE NEXT STEP

Understanding your partner's specific dialect of quality time can make every shared moment more meaningful. Do they love the spontaneity of improvising, the stability of managing, the intention behind planning, or the vision of dreaming together? **The 5 Love Languages Premium Assessment** is designed to help you uncover these nuances, offering personalized insights into how your partner experiences love through time spent together. It's a simple way to ensure that your time isn't just shared—it's truly connecting.

Take the Premium Assessment today and learn how to create moments of quality time that speak directly to your partner's heart.

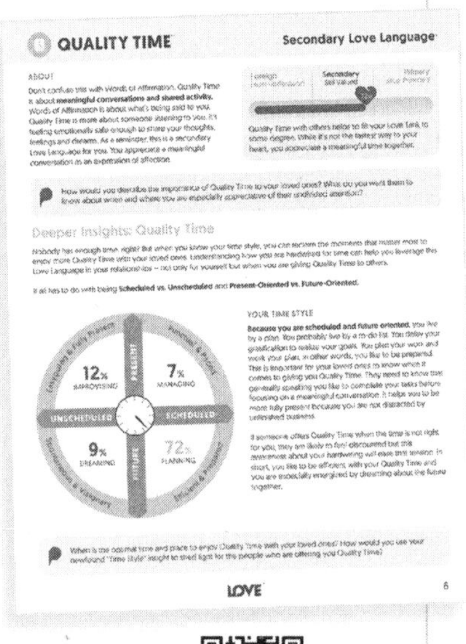

5LoveLanguages.com/Premium

CHAPTER 9

Receiving Gifts

Unwrapping the Perfect Treasure

"Babe, Christmas is coming up," she said casually while sitting cross-legged on the couch, scrolling through her phone.

"Uh-huh," he replied cautiously from the kitchen, where he was pretending to focus on unloading the dishwasher. He could already feel the pressure building.

"I just want you to know," she continued, her tone breezy but calculated, "I'm not really into gifts this year. Let's just keep it simple."

He froze, a single plate in his hand, and turned to look at her. "Define 'simple,'" he said slowly, his eyebrows arching. "Because last time you said 'simple,' I bought you socks, and . . . well, that didn't go so well."

"Simple doesn't mean thoughtless," she shot back, looking up from her phone. "It means meaningful. Like, I don't need anything expensive or flashy."

"Okay . . . so, meaningful but not expensive. Got it," he said, resuming his task and muttering under his breath.

"And no gift cards," she added, almost as an afterthought, scrolling again as if she hadn't just detonated his backup plan.

He sighed loudly, closing the dishwasher with a clang. "There goes Plan A."

She smiled sweetly, tilting her head as if to soften the blow. "It's not that hard. You just have to know me well enough to pick something that shows you've been paying attention."

He dropped the dish towel onto the counter and leaned against it, crossing his arms. "Right, because that's not pressure at all."

"And nothing practical," she added, her eyes flicking up at him to gauge his reaction.

"Wait, so…not expensive, not flashy, not practical, and no gift cards?"

"That's right."

"So am I supposed to hand-craft you a poem on paper I made from tree bark I harvested?"

She raised an eyebrow, deadpan. "Don't make promises you can't keep."

He groaned, dragging a hand down his face, but couldn't help the smile creeping in. This was their dance—a tug-of-war between her playful, layered expectations and his sometimes overly literal approach to love.

If your partner's love language is receiving gifts, this might sound familiar. After all, gift-giving is a delicate art. You already know from reading *The 5 Love Languages* that it's not about the price tag—it's about showing thoughtfulness, attention, and care. And while the process might feel intimidating (or downright confusing), it's ultimately about the heart behind the gesture. In this chapter, we'll explore what makes a gift truly meaningful to your partner.

A Quick Review

Receiving gifts is about the thought behind the gesture. It's not about the monetary value—it's about the meaning and care that went into the gift itself. For someone whose heart resonates with this love language, receiving a gift is a tangible reminder that they're seen, valued, and loved.

Ways to Practice **Receiving Gifts**

- *Bringing them a book that reminded you of a conversation you had together.*
- *Picking up their favorite snack or drink on your way home, just because you thought of them.*
- *Surprising them with tickets to a show, concert, or experience they've been wanting to attend.*
- *Creating a personalized playlist or photo album that captures special memories.*
- *Choosing a unique souvenir from a trip that reflects their interests or passions.*

Again, for those who thrive on receiving gifts, it's not the size or cost of the gift that matters—it's the thoughtfulness and intentionality behind it. These tokens of affection are physical representations of love, care, and attention.

As we delve deeper into understanding the nuances of this love language, you'll learn how to personalize your gift giving and move beyond traditional presents, finding ways to speak to your partner's heart through meaningful, creative gestures.

Why Receiving Gifts Speaks Straight to the Heart

While gifts can bring joy to anyone, for some they represent far more than the item itself. Early experiences often shape this love language—growing up in environments where gifts were either cherished or overlooked influences how we associate tangible tokens with love. Whether filling a gap or building on a tradition, gifts become enduring symbols of care and attention.

Culturally, gifts have long been a universal symbol of affection and appreciation, carrying meaning beyond their material value. A well-chosen gift says, "I know you, I've thought about you, and you matter to me." For the recipient, it's not about the expense—it's about the intentionality and personal connection behind it.

Those who are drawn to this love language are deeply attuned to the thought behind the gift. The gift often symbolizes presence and connection, especially for those who may have experienced emotional or physical absence in their early relationships. For these individuals, a meaningful gift can reinforce a sense of being seen and valued. For others who grew up with consistent expressions of love through gifts, the tradition strengthens their sense of security and belonging.

Personality traits, as always, can amplify the impact of this love language. Individuals with an eye for detail or a strong sense of sentimentality often treasure gifts as a tangible reminder of the giver's love and thoughtfulness. For them, a carefully selected gift can evoke deep emotions, serving as a lasting symbol of the relationship.

For someone who resonates with receiving gifts, it's not about quantity or extravagance—it's about the meaning and care embedded in the gesture. A gift, no matter how small, speaks volumes, reminding them that they're cherished and always in the giver's thoughts.

When Receiving Gifts Matters Most

Receiving gifts is always meaningful for someone with this love language, but there are moments when it holds even deeper significance.

Times of Celebration

Birthdays, anniversaries, promotions, or holidays, are, of course, opportunities to make the person with this love language feel uniquely valued. These occasions often carry heightened expectations because the gift symbolizes more than the event itself. It reflects how well you know them and your ability to honor them.

You already know that neglecting to acknowledge these milestones with a meaningful gift can leave them feeling overlooked or undervalued.

Times of Difficulty

During times of hardship—such as an illness, a loss, or a stressful period—gifts take on a new level of meaning. A small gesture, like a care package, their favorite treat, or even a handwritten note paired with a meaningful item, can offer comfort and reassurance.

For example: "I know you've been feeling overwhelmed, so I stopped by Starbucks and picked up your favorite—an extra-hot caramel macchiato with a splash of oat milk and a dash of cinnamon on top. And I couldn't resist grabbing that double-chocolate brownie you love because I figured it might make this tough season a little sweeter." This small act shows that you've paid attention to the little details that bring them comfort.

Times of Spontaneity

Unexpected gifts given "just because" can hold extraordinary meaning for someone whose love language is receiving gifts. These moments show that you don't need a reason or an occasion to think of them—they're on your mind simply because they're important to you.

A surprise, like bringing home their favorite lavender-scented bath salts with a small note that says, "Take some time to relax—you deserve it," communicates, "You're always in my heart."

When Not to Focus on Receiving Gifts

You might think that if your partner loves receiving gifts, you should keep them coming. Not so. There are moments when focusing on gift-giving can feel shallow, inappropriate, or even counterproductive. Recognizing when not to give is as important as understanding the value of thoughtful giving. Gifts should come from a place of genuine care and connection—offering them at the wrong time or for the wrong reasons can undermine their meaning.

For example, avoid giving gifts as a substitute for emotional connection. If your partner is feeling hurt or distant, presenting a gift without addressing the underlying issue can seem like an attempt to buy forgiveness or gloss over the problem. In these moments, a heartfelt conversation or another love language may be a better way to rebuild trust.

Generally speaking, a gift as a peace offering is not recommended —"Here, I got this for you. Can we move on now?" That's sure to feel manipulative or insincere. Instead, resolve the conflict first so that any gifts exchanged later can feel like genuine expressions of love rather than a tool to win someone over.

Timing also matters when it comes to special occasions. If your partner values thoughtfulness, giving a gift that seems rushed, generic, or disconnected from their preferences can feel like a missed opportunity rather than a meaningful gesture. For example, you should think twice about giving a kitchen appliance if they've expressed a desire for something sentimental.

Finally, gifts can backfire if they come with strings attached. If your partner feels pressure to reciprocate or meet an expectation because of your gift, it may create tension instead of joy. Gifts should always feel like a free, no-obligation expression of love.

Understanding when not to focus on receiving gifts ensures that the moments you do give will feel authentic, intentional, and truly impactful. Sometimes, stepping back from gifting allows other forms of love to shine brighter.

How Receiving Gifts Can Get Lost in Translation

Not all gifts land the way we intend. Even with the best intentions, our efforts to show love through gifts can sometimes leave our partner feeling misunderstood or unappreciated. This happens when we overlook their preferences, the context of the gift, or the thoughtfulness they expect.

One common issue is choosing a gift that feels impersonal. While you might see a box of Ghirardelli chocolates as a perfectly acceptable gesture on Valentine's Day, your partner may see it as last-minute panic buy that screams, "I forgot what day it was until I overheard someone at work talking about it."

A gift can also fall flat when it doesn't align with your partner's tastes or needs. For instance, surprising them with something you think they should want—like a fitness tracker when they've never once mentioned wanting to track their steps—can feel less like love and more like, "Here's a gentle nudge to go for a jog."

Finally, gifts lose their impact when they're overshadowed by expectations. If your partner feels pressured to respond with excessive gratitude or reciprocate with a gift of equal value, the joy of the gesture is diminished. A true gift should be freely given, with no strings attached.

And of course, there's one more way receiving gifts can miss the mark: not understanding your partner's dialect. That deserves a closer look.

Discovering the Dialects of Receiving Gifts

You might be thinking, *A gift is a gift.* But receiving gifts, like any love language, has its own distinct dialects—different ways of expressing love through tangible expression. Not all gifts resonate in the same way, and understanding your partner's unique gift dialect can make all the difference.

There are four primary dialects of receiving gifts: **fanciful**, **functional**, **sensible**, and **sentimental**. Each represents a distinct approach to giving that results from whether your partner's gift dialect is simple or extravagant and whether it is more heartfelt or practical. This diagram helps:

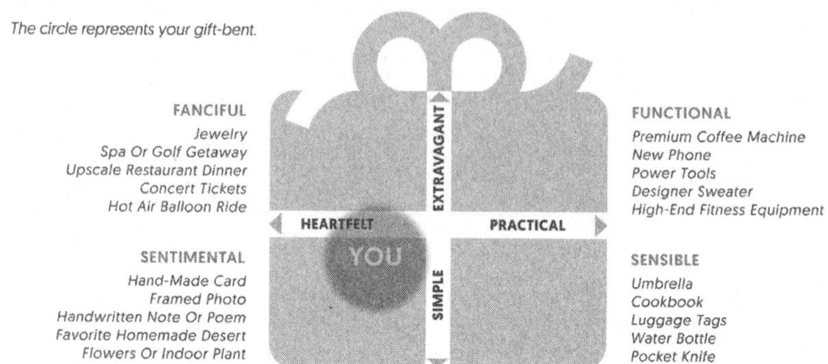

By discovering which of these four possibilities speaks most clearly to your partner, you can ensure your gifts feel intentional, personal, and deeply appreciated.

In the sections ahead, we'll explore these four dialects, helping you unlock the art of giving in a way that truly connects with your partner's heart.

RECEIVING GIFTS DIALECT #1

Fanciful Gifts

This is all about heartfelt extravagance. For those who connect with this dialect, the joy of receiving comes from the creativity, thoughtfulness, and over-the-top effort behind the gesture. It's not about the practicality of the gift—it's about the delight of being surprised by something extraordinary and unexpected.

Fanciful gifts capture the imagination and make the recipient feel cherished in a way that's bold and celebratory. Whether it's a bouquet of their favorite flowers delivered "just because," tickets to a dream destination, or an elaborate piece of jewelry, these gifts convey love through their sense of wonder and excitement.

Embracing the fanciful dialect doesn't mean you need to max out your credit cards or book a private jet. Extravagance isn't about the price tag. It's about the thoughtful creativity behind it. A handwritten love letter tied with an elaborate ribbon is fanciful because of the presentation. A surprise picnic with special treats under the stars can feel just as fanciful as anything you'd find at Tiffany's. The key is to think outside the box, not break the bank. After all, the most fanciful gifts are often the ones that make your partner feel like you've gone the extra mile—without actually needing to apply for a second mortgage.

They simply like the feeling of being swept up in the moment. It's about the gesture being big enough to say, "You're worth the effort, and I wanted to make this as special as you are."

Are Fanciful Gifts Your Partner's Dialect?

Does your partner love creative gifts that are not ordinary? Do they appreciate gestures that show you've put extra thought and effort into making them feel special? If their favorite gifts tend to have an element of surprise and excitement, Fanciful may be their receiving gifts dialect.

You know fanciful gifts are your partner's dialect if:

- ☐ They get excited by elaborate surprises, like a romantic dinner reservation or tickets to an unexpected event.
- ☐ They cherish gifts that feel unique, imaginative, or hard to come by.

- ☐ They often comment on how much they appreciate the extra thought or creativity behind a gift.
- ☐ They enjoy gifts that feel celebratory, like flowers, balloons, or anything that adds a touch of drama to the moment.
- ☐ They seem most moved when a gift creates a memorable experience, not just an object.
- ☐ They love when a gift feels like it was designed especially for them—whether it's customized, personalized, or tailored to their tastes.
- ☐ They frequently talk about gifts from the past that made them feel swept off their feet or deeply seen.

If this list sounds like your partner, fanciful is likely their primary dialect. For someone who values this approach, the magic of a gift lies in how much thought and care went into making it feel special.

Roland and Patricia had been married five years. Every birthday, he gave her something practical—a skillet, a handheld vacuum, a carving knife—because that's how he showed love: giving what she needed. Patricia always said "Thank you" but never looked thrilled.

This year, Roland decided to try something different. He knew Patricia loved art, so he asked a friend—a painter—to create a portrait of her. It cost more than he'd usually spend, but it felt right.

On her birthday, after dessert at a nice restaurant, the waiter returned with a wrapped frame. "One more treat for you," he said.

Patricia peeled back the paper and gasped. Her eyes sparkled. Her smile widened. She stood and said, "You did this for me? I never expected something like this. It's beautiful. I love you."

Without knowing it, Roland had just spoken Patricia's love language of gifts—in her favorite dialect: thoughtful, personal, and from the heart.

Why Fanciful Gifts Matter

Fashion designer Christian Dior is attributed with saying, "Happiness is the secret to all beauty. There is no beauty without happiness."[15] For someone who values fanciful gifts, the happiness they feel in receiving something extravagant becomes its own kind of beauty—an expression of love that is as bold and celebratory as it is thoughtful.

A fanciful gift shows your partner that you see them as special and worth the extra effort to surprise and amaze. What makes fanciful gifts so impactful is the thoughtfulness behind them. It's not about the extravagance itself—it's about the *feeling* that the gift creates. These gifts say, "I know you and I want to give you something that feels extraordinary."

Fanciful gifts matter because they add a sense of magic to your relationship. They break up the routine and remind your partner of the joy, creativity, and fun that love brings. For those who value this dialect, these gestures aren't about showing off—they're about showing how deeply you care in the most imaginative and heartfelt way possible.

RECEIVING GIFTS DIALECT #2

Functional Gifts

The functional dialect of receiving gifts is all about practicality wrapped in thoughtfulness that creates an impact. These gifts are not only useful but also show that you've been paying attention to what your partner needs or values in their day-to-day life. For someone who resonates with this dialect, the perfect gift is one that solves a problem, improves their routine, or makes life easier—all while still carrying a sense of care and intention.

Functional gifts might include something like a high-quality coffee maker for their morning brew, a stylish yet durable backpack for their commute, or even a set of noise-canceling headphones for their busy workdays. While these gifts are practical at their core, they go beyond utility by demonstrating your understanding of what will truly enhance their life.

For someone who values this dialect, a functional gift says, "I see you, I understand what makes your life easier or better, and I want to support you." It's a balance of thoughtfulness and practicality that shows love in a way that's both meaningful and impactful.

Are Functional Gifts Your Partner's Dialect?

Does your partner love gifts that are both thoughtful and useful? Do they light up when you give them something that makes their daily life easier or more efficient? If they appreciate gifts that combine practicality with intention, functional might be their receiving gifts dialect.

You know functional gifts are your partner's dialect if:

- ☐ They get excited when a gift solves a problem or fulfills a need they've mentioned (like a new phone).
- ☐ They appreciate high-quality, durable items that are built to last.
- ☐ They often comment on how much they love a gift they can use regularly, like a kitchen gadget or a work accessory.
- ☐ They're more impressed by thoughtful practicality than flashy or purely decorative items.
- ☐ They frequently express gratitude for gifts that make their life easier, whether it's something small or a larger investment.
- ☐ They value gifts that reflect their lifestyle or hobbies, like a tool for their favorite craft or an item that enhances their workspace.
- ☐ They often say things like, "This is exactly what I needed!" when receiving a gift.

If this list resonates with your partner, functional is likely their primary gift dialect. And if you're cringing a bit because this dialect often comes with a literal price tag, we want to ease your concerns. Sure, functional gifts can sometimes come with a higher price tag, a high-quality coffee maker or a durable set of tools, for example. But they are not a routine gift.

In other words, you don't have to break the bank every month to speak this dialect. These bigger gifts are special and out of the ordinary. Thoughtful and affordable options—like a clever kitchen gadget, a handy organizer, or even a personalized calendar—can show just as much care and attention. The key is a gift that aligns with your partner's needs and lifestyle. So save the big-ticket gifts for truly special occasions.

Zach and Tessa had been married just under three years. They were still figuring out careers, routines, and how to keep the laundry from taking over their lives. But one thing Zach had learned early on: Tessa's love language was receiving gifts.

Not the "roses and diamonds" kind—though she liked a surprise now and then. What really lit her up were gifts that made her life easier.

Lately, Tessa had been working from home—and struggling to stay focused. Between neighbors mowing their lawns and Zach clattering dishes in the kitchen, she kept mentioning how hard it was to concentrate during Zoom calls.

One afternoon, Zach was at a coffee shop and saw a pair of top-rated noise-canceling headphones on sale. He thought, *This is it.*

He bought them, wrapped them in brown paper, and left the package on her desk with a sticky note: "For your sanity. Love, Z."

Later that day, Tessa texted him: "You are a genius. I actually got through my meeting without hearing the leaf blower. I might cry."

Zach grinned. Mission accomplished.

To an outsider, it might have looked like just a pair of headphones.

But to Tessa, it was a love note—written in tech.

That's the functional dialect. When gifts are chosen not just for what they *are*, but for what they *do*—how they support, ease, or empower someone you love. For Tessa, it wasn't about being spoiled. It was about being seen.

Why Functional Gifts Matter

For someone who values this dialect, these gifts aren't just things—they're solutions, tools, and enhancements that bring ease, efficiency, or enjoyment to their daily routine. What makes functional gifts so meaningful is their ability to say, "I see you, and I care about what matters to you." A well-chosen functional gift reflects attention to detail and demonstrates that you've been listening to their needs or noticing what could make their life smoother.

These gifts also carry a lasting impact. While other gifts may fade with time, a functional one gets used and appreciated again and again, serving as a consistent reminder of your love and care. We know of a husband who has carried the same embossed leather satchel that his wife gave him twenty years ago! For someone who values this dialect, functional gifts aren't just practical—they're powerful symbols of support and understanding.

RECEIVING GIFTS DIALECT #3

Sensible Gifts

This is all about practicality and simplicity. These gifts are thoughtful in their usefulness but don't aim to be flashy or extravagant. For someone who resonates with this dialect, the best gifts are those that meet a need or serve a clear purpose, showing care through their practicality rather than their price or presentation.

Sensible gifts might include everyday essentials like a cozy pair of socks, a planner to help them stay organized, or a new coffee mug to replace their worn-out favorite. These gifts may seem understated, but for someone who values this dialect, they represent attention to detail and an understanding of what truly matters in their day-to-day life.

For those who appreciate sensible gifts, it's not about making a big statement—it's about showing love through thoughtful, simple gestures that quietly make life a little better.

Are Sensible Gifts Your Partner's Dialect?

Does your partner seem most grateful for gifts that serve a clear purpose in their daily life? Something small and simple? If they value usefulness over extravagance, sensible might be their receiving gifts dialect.

You know sensible gifts are your partner's dialect if:

- ☐ They appreciate everyday essentials, like a warm blanket, a favorite brand of coffee, or a new water bottle.
- ☐ They often mention how much they love gifts that are practical and immediately useful.
- ☐ They're less impressed by extravagant gestures and more touched by thoughtful, low-key gifts that show you're paying attention.
- ☐ They prefer quality over quantity, valuing a well-chosen item over something purely decorative or flashy.
- ☐ They often express gratitude for gifts that improve their routine, even in small ways.
- ☐ They frequently mention how much they appreciate the thoughtfulness of "just the right thing" rather than an over-the-top gesture.
- ☐ They enjoy gifts that feel personal but not showy, reflecting their preference for simplicity and practicality.

Does this list resonate with your partner? If so, sensible is likely their primary gift dialect. For someone who values this approach, the perfect gift doesn't have to be big or bold—it just needs to show that you've thought about what makes their life a little easier or more comfortable.

William could never keep track of the birthdays of their five children and twenty-four grandchildren. So, his wife gave him a unique "remembrance gift." On New Year's Day, she synced a shared digital calendar to his phone—with every birthday listed, along with each person's current age.

He was touched. "I'm going to call each one on their birthday," he said. That simple gesture sparked a turning point in his connection with his kids and grandkids.

The following January, she updated the calendar and sent him a fresh version. William smiled and said, "This is one of the best gifts you've ever given me." He repeated that sentiment for years.

It was thoughtful, tech-savvy, and deeply meaningful—a digital gift that helped him stay close to the people who mattered most.

Why Sensible Gifts Matter

For someone who values this dialect, it's not about extravagance or fanfare—it's about the thoughtfulness behind giving something that fits seamlessly into their life. These gifts quietly say, "I see you and care about what makes your day-to-day a little easier."

For someone who values sensible gifts, extravagance can feel unnecessary or even uncomfortable. They may prefer that money be spent wisely or saved for something more meaningful. Lavish gifts might leave them feeling guilty or misunderstood.

The beauty of sensible gifts is in their simplicity. A cozy pair of slippers, a set of their favorite pens, or a well-loved household item replaced at just the right time can have a deeper impact than something flashy.

It's not the size or price of the gift that counts, but how well it reflects your understanding of what they value.

Sensible gifts also serve as practical reminders of your care. Every time your partner uses or enjoys the gift, they're reminded of your love and thoughtfulness. For someone who values this dialect, a simple, useful gesture can speak volumes—showing that love doesn't have to be complicated to be deeply meaningful.

RECEIVING GIFTS DIALECT #4

Sentimental Gifts

This dialect is all about heartfelt simplicity. These gifts hold emotional significance. They show your partner that you truly understand and cherish them. More than any of the four gift dialects, this one is the least concerned about monetary value. It's all about personal meaning.

Sentimental gifts might include a framed photo of a special memory, a handwritten letter, or an item that represents a shared experience or inside joke. It could be something as simple as a pressed flower from a meaningful walk, a playlist of songs tied to your relationship, or a memento from your first date. These gestures are small but deeply personal, reflecting the unique bond you share.

For someone who values this dialect, a sentimental gift says, "I treasure the moments we've shared." It's not about the gift itself—it's about the emotions and memories it carries.

Are Sentimental Gifts Your Partner's Dialect?

Does your partner like gifts that are deeply personal, tied to a memory, or carry emotional significance? If they value gifts that reflect your unique connection, sentimental may be their primary receiving gifts dialect.

You know sentimental gifts are your partner's dialect if:

- ☐ They treasure gifts that commemorate a meaningful event, like a keepsake from a special trip or a memento from a milestone moment.
- ☐ They're deeply moved by personalized items, such as engraved jewelry, a scrapbook, or a handwritten letter.
- ☐ They love when gifts reflect inside jokes that only the two of you understand.
- ☐ They value thought and effort far more than monetary cost.
- ☐ They're more likely to keep and cherish gifts that feel symbolic of your relationship than something purely practical.
- ☐ They reminisce about gifts from the past that had emotional significance.
- ☐ They love gifts that involve an element of surprise and thoughtfulness, like a note hidden in a book they're reading or a song dedicated to them.

Would your partner check a lot of these boxes? If so, Sentimental is probably their primary gift dialect. For someone who values this approach, the best gifts aren't the most expensive—they're the ones that hold the most meaning.

One of the most meaningful gifts my wife, Karolyn, gave me years ago still travels with me every time I speak around the world. It's nothing fancy—just a handwritten note on a sheet of notebook paper. But it means the world to me.

My Sweet Gary!

I do Love you.
I shall pray for you.
I am so blessed to live with you.

I am "proud" of <u>you</u>.
(thankful)
(excited)
(Biblical Proud)
Grateful
Life with <u>you</u> is beyond belief.
Have fun – bear fruit.
Enjoy and return.
Stay warm.
K

Sentimental gifts, spoken in the right dialect, can keep on giving for years to come!

Why Sentimental Gifts Matter

Gifts in this dialect don't just show love—they tell a story, one that celebrates your connection and honors the moments that have shaped your relationship. These gifts resonate on a deeper psychological level because they tap into our innate need to feel seen, remembered, and cherished. They speak directly to the heart by acknowledging the emotional significance of shared experiences.

What makes sentimental gifts so impactful is that they aren't about extravagance or practicality—they're about meaning. A sentimental gift reflects emotional attunement. It's a way of saying, "I treasure the memories we've created together." These gifts reinforce a sense of belonging and connection, which is a core need in any close relationship.

Sentimental gifts matter because they transform ordinary objects into extraordinary symbols of love and intimacy. For someone who values this dialect, these tokens become touchstones for cherished memories, evoking feelings of joy, gratitude, and togetherness every time they're seen or held. They create a lasting connection that transcends the gift itself.

When it comes to receiving gifts, we've explored the four most meaningful dialects of this love language: fanciful, functional, sensible, and sentimental gifts. Each one carries its own unique impact. While there are countless ways to express this love language, these four capture the essence of what truly matters. And, of course, your partner may speak all these dialects over time. But they are likely to have a go-to favorite. The key is discovering which one resonates most with your partner.

Speaking of that, giving gifts is a wonderful way to show love, but too much focus on the "wow factor" can sometimes overshadow the personal connection your partner craves. That's what leads to an "overload."

Avoiding Receiving Gifts Overload

Gift-giving is a great way to show love, but it's surprisingly easy to go overboard. If every occasion or random Tuesday afternoon comes with a present, your partner might start feeling like they're on the receiving end of a never-ending QVC marathon. For someone who values receiving gifts, it's not about how much you give or how often—it's about the thought and meaning behind each one. A meaningful gift says "I know you," while a constant stream of stuff might start to feel like, "I just couldn't stop shopping."

To avoid gift overload, focus on the why behind the gift rather than just the act of giving. A single meaningful present—like something tied to a shared memory or a small token that speaks to their personality—will always outweigh a steady stream of generic gestures. Think quality over quantity: a hand-picked memento says "I see you," while a flood of random knick-knacks might say, "I couldn't stop myself."

It's also worth keeping an eye on your partner's response. If they start joking about needing a storage unit or re-gifting your offerings, it might be time to pump the brakes. Gifts should enhance your connection, not overwhelm it. By saving your gifts for the moments that truly matter, you ensure they remain impactful, memorable, and a genuine expression of love—without the risk of gift fatigue.

Gift-giving is one of the oldest human traditions, a way we've expressed love, gratitude, and devotion for millennia. As said the saying goes, "People will forget what you said, people will forget what you did, but people will never forget how you made them feel."[16] For those whose love language is receiving gifts, the right gift is a tangible way to create an unforgettable feeling with a tangible reminder that they are cherished.

While this might not apply to the waffle maker you panic-bought last Christmas, it does speak to every fanciful, functional, sensible, or sentimental gift that comes from a loving heart. When done thoughtfully, gifts become more than things—they become reflections of the love you carry inside.

So, whether you're planning your next holiday surprise or just looking for a way to say "I love you" on a random Tuesday, remember: the best gifts aren't found in a store—they're found in the heart. And if all else fails, you can always write that poem . . . you know, the one on tree-bark paper you harvested, pressed, and handcrafted into a scroll.

TAKE THE NEXT STEP

Discovering your partner's unique dialect of receiving gifts will deepen your connection and take the guesswork out of gift-giving. And the **5 Love Languages Premium Assessment** is designed to help you uncover these specific preferences, giving you personalized insights into how your partner experiences love through gifts. It's a practical tool that ensures your next gift is one they'll truly cherish—because it speaks their language. Take the Premium Assessment today and unlock a deeper understanding of how to give gifts that leave a lasting impression.

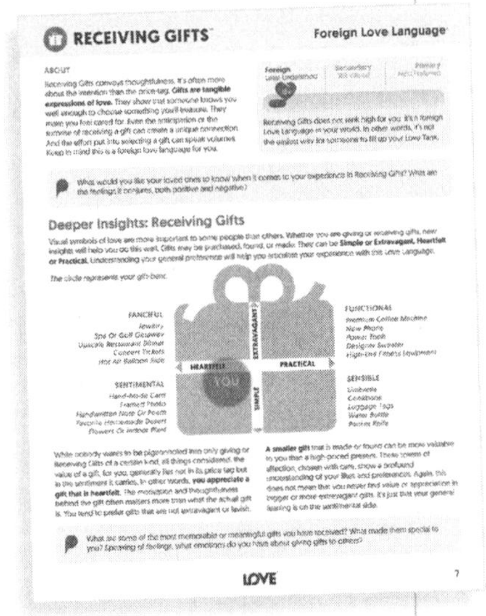

RECEIVING GIFTS™

Foreign Love Language

ABOUT

Receiving Gifts conveys thoughtfulness. It's often more about the intention than the price tag. **Gifts are tangible expressions of love.** They show that someone knows you well enough to choose something you'll treasure. They make you feel cared for. Even the anticipation or the surprise of receiving a gift can create a unique connection. And the effort put into selecting a gift can speak volumes. Keep in mind this is a foreign love language for you.

Receiving Gifts does not rank high for you. It's a foreign Love Language in your world. In other words, it's not the easiest way for someone to fill up your Love Tank.

What would you like your loved ones to know when it comes to your experience in Receiving Gifts? What are the feelings it conjures, both positive and negative?

Deeper Insights: Receiving Gifts

Visual symbols of love are more important to some people than others. Whether you are giving or receiving gifts, new insights will help you do this well. Gifts may be purchased, found, or made. They can be **Simple or Extravagant, Heartfelt or Practical.** Understanding your general preference will help you articulate your experience with this Love Language.

The circle represents your gifts bent.

While nobody wants to be pigeonholed into only giving or Receiving Gifts of a certain kind, all things considered, the value of a gift, for you, generally lies not in its price tag but in the sentiment it carries. In other words, **you appreciate a gift that is heartfelt.** The motivation and thoughtfulness behind the gift often matters more than what the actual gift is. You tend to prefer gifts that are not extravagant or lavish.

A smaller gift that is made or found can be more valuable to you than a high-priced present. These tokens of affection, chosen with care, show a profound understanding of your likes and preferences. Again, this does not mean that you never find value or appreciation in bigger or more extravagant gifts. It's just that your general leaning is on the sentimental side.

What are some of the most memorable or meaningful gifts you have received? What made them special to you? Speaking of feelings, what emotions do you have about giving gifts to others?

LOVE 7

5LoveLanguages.com/Premium

CHAPTER 10

Acts of Service

Transforming the Mundane into Meaning

The Vic Theater in Chicago is packed, buzzing with the kind of energy only comedian Seth Meyers can inspire. The audience—loyal fans who've followed him from *Saturday Night Live*'s Weekend Update desk to the comfy chairs of *Late Night with Seth Meyers*—is ready for his sharp wit and self-deprecating humor. Tonight, he's talking love, marriage, and, surprisingly, *The 5 Love Languages*.

Seth kicks things off with the setup: "Do you guys know the concept of love languages?" he asks the crowd. A murmur of agreement ripples through the theater, peppered with a few nervous chuckles from the men in the audience who clearly don't. "Here's the concept of love languages for those of you who don't know," he explains. "There are five love languages. This is how people receive love: acts of service, touch, quality time, gifts, and words of encouragement."

He pauses, scanning the crowd, his expression morphing into faux disbelief. "And, guys, I don't know who came up with this list. All I know is that their love language is definitely acts of service, because this is the biggest scam ever—that acts of service is lumped on this list with the other four *reasonable* things."

The crowd roars. Seth knows exactly how to hook them, revealing that this is his wife's love language. He launches into a routine about how much harder acts of service is compared to the others.

"Here's life if your love language is touch and your wife's is acts of service," he says. "'When I get home, I would like a hug.' 'I need you to fix the boiler.'" The audience bursts out laughing as he continues, "Quality time? 'Want to go for a walk?' 'Yeah, after you clean out the gutters.'"

Seth delivers the punchline with perfect timing, hands gesturing as if he's laying out the terms of a raw deal: "It's like if an airline's loyalty program was like, we have gold, platinum, silver . . . and when we land, *you clean the plane.*"

It's the kind of insight Seth is known for—smart, relatable, and enough of an exaggeration to make it hilarious. He has a way of turning the mundane struggles of marriage into comedy gold. In this case, he's hit on a little bit of a truth, at least for those whose native tongue is not acts of service: this love language is no small task.

It's actually a series of small tasks.

Sure, acts of service *does* demand effort—it may not seem as simple as giving a compliment or spending a quiet moment together. It requires intentional action, and sometimes a certain amount of sweat equity.

But we want to assure you of another truth: acts of service aren't nearly as daunting as fixing the boiler or scaling a ladder to clean the gutters. Like the other love languages, it's about the heart behind the action. It's the small, thoughtful gestures—like making your partner's morning coffee, picking up their dry cleaning without being asked, or quietly refueling their car so they don't have to—that truly make an impact. These acts don't require grand gestures or extraordinary skills. They're simply about noticing what your partner needs and stepping in to make their day a little easier. In that sense, acts of service aren't a burden—they're the most powerful way to say "I love you" to a partner that speaks this language.

A Quick Review

Acts of service is about actions speaking louder than words. It's about doing something tangible to lighten your partner's load or make their life easier. For the person whose heart resonates with this language, small acts of service aren't just helpful—they're essential to feeling valued and loved.

Ways to Practice **Acts of Service**

- *Taking the time to warm up their car on a chilly morning before they leave for work.*
- *Fixing that squeaky door they've been mentioning for weeks, without being asked.*
- *Bringing them coffee in bed, exactly the way they like it.*
- *Researching and scheduling an appointment they've been putting off, like the dentist or car maintenance.*
- *Running an errand they've been dreading, like picking up a package or returning something to the store.*

These actions, as simple as they may seem, have a profound impact on someone whose love language is acts of service, especially when they're done with intention and without expectation of something in return. For them, these efforts go beyond chores or gestures—they represent love, care, and the willingness to prioritize their well-being.

As we explore how to tailor this love language to your partner's personal dialect, you'll learn to move beyond routine tasks and find creative ways to transform the mundane into meaningful expressions of love.

Why Acts of Service Speaks Straight to the Heart

Acts of service meet a deep human need for support and security. While everyone appreciates a helping hand, for some, actions speak much louder than any words could. Early experiences often shape this love language. Growing up in environments where acts of service were either abundant or absent influences how we associate love with tangible efforts. Acts of service can communicate care, dedication, and selflessness in a uniquely powerful way.

Psychologically, individuals drawn to this love language are highly attuned to effort and follow-through. The role of reliability in forming emotional bonds is backed up by stacks of research. For those who experienced inconsistency or neglect in childhood, acts of service can rebuild a sense of trust and stability. And for those raised with dependable caretakers, acts of service can convey reassurance and comfort in the consistency of thoughtful actions.

On a behavioral level, acts of service demonstrate prioritization. To the recipient, these efforts aren't just about getting things checked off their to-do list—they're proof that their well-being is valued. Small gestures, like anticipating their needs or completing an unspoken request, signal that their partner is paying attention and willing to step in without being asked.

Personality traits, of course, also play a role. Dependable and detail-oriented individuals may see acts of service as a natural way to express and receive love, while those who value structure and organization may find deep comfort in actions that reduce chaos or lighten their load. For some, these actions restore order and create a sense of balance, which is inherently calming.

For someone whose love language is acts of service, it's not about the size of the gesture—it's about the intentionality and thought behind it. Actions that ease their burdens, no matter how small, speak directly to their heart, communicating care, respect, and love in the most practical and meaningful way.

When Acts of Service Matter Most

Acts of service are always meaningful to the person who speaks this love language, but there are moments when they become especially significant.

Times of High Demand

During pressured times with looming deadlines or intense workloads, an act of service can feel like a lifeline. Failing to offer practical help during overwhelming times can leave them feeling unseen or unsupported, but stepping in communicates that their well-being is your priority.

For example, surprising them by taking over what they typically handle, like grocery shopping, meal prepping for the week ahead, scheduling the kids' appointments, or tackling the laundry pile, says, "I see how hard you're working, and I want to take some of the burden off."

Times of Transition

During major life changes—such as moving, starting a new job, or welcoming a baby—acts of service become a vital expression of love. These transitions often bring new challenges, and your willingness to step in and share the load reinforces that you're a team.

For instance: organizing the chaos of a move by unpacking the kitchen while they focus on settling into their new workspace can show them, "I'm with you in this, and I'm here to make things easier." Acts of service during transitions demonstrate your commitment to their happiness during a season of uncertainty.

Times of Illness or Fatigue

When someone is physically or emotionally drained—whether from illness, injury, or simple exhaustion—acts of service provide comfort and care in a way words cannot.

For example: running a warm bath and setting out fresh towels, or leaving a cup of herbal tea on the counter with a note that says, "Rest and recharge—I've got everything else covered tonight." These acts of care go beyond the practical; they show empathy and a willingness to go out of your way to meet their needs.

When Not to Focus on Acts of Service

While acts of service can be deeply meaningful, there are moments when focusing on them may feel misplaced or overwhelming. You need to know when to pause as much as when to step in. Like all love languages, acts of service should always come from a place of thoughtfulness and consideration.

For example, avoid doing something for your partner that they enjoy doing themselves. If they find satisfaction or relaxation in tackling certain tasks, stepping in without asking could feel less like help and more like interference. So ask yourself if you're overstepping.

Another time to be cautious is if the gesture carries an unspoken expectation of gratitude or reciprocity. That's likely to leave your partner feeling pressured rather than loved. For example, washing their car and then later commenting, "I went out of my way to do something nice—don't you think I deserve a little appreciation?" can make the act feel more like an obligation than love.

It's also important to be mindful of boundaries. Offering help when it hasn't been asked for, or repeatedly insisting on doing something your partner has declined, can feel intrusive or dismissive of their independence. For example, insisting on organizing their workspace after they've said they prefer to do it themselves can come across as overstepping, even if well-intentioned. Respecting their autonomy shows love in a different but equally meaningful way.

Understanding when not to focus on acts of service ensures that your efforts will feel thoughtful and appreciated rather than misaligned or forced. Pausing at the right moments allows you to approach this love language with sensitivity, making your actions more meaningful when the time is right.

How Acts of Service Can Get Lost in Translation

Even with the best of intentions, our efforts to show love through actions can sometimes leave our partner feeling more frustrated than supported. This happens when we fail to consider their preferences, timing, or the true purpose behind our actions.

One common issue is performing a task they don't actually want done. For instance, cleaning out their closet and donating some of their clothes to Goodwill—without asking—might feel less like help and more like a personal ambush. For someone who values this love language, the key is offering support that aligns with their needs, not just your assumptions (or your opinion about how many hoodies one person needs).

Another way acts of service can miss the mark is when they come across as performative. For example, loudly declaring, "I'm doing the dishes tonight, like I *always* do," might get the sink cleared, but it also turns your act of love into a one-person awards show for "Martyr of the Year."

Timing is also critical. Trying to offer help when your partner is in the middle of something important—like starting to mow the lawn while they're having a serious phone conversation outside—might leave them feeling more interrupted than cared for. Pausing to ask, "How can I help?" before diving in can make all the difference.

Finally, acts of service can lose their impact when they're given with an unspoken expectation of acknowledgment. If your partner senses that your effort is more about receiving praise—"Did you notice I vacuumed the entire house?"—it might feel less like love and more like a plea for validation.

And of course, there's one more way acts of service can miss the mark: neglecting their personal dialect. That's worth a closer look.

Discovering the Dialects of Acts of Service

Like all love languages, acts of service has distinct dialects—specific and personalized ways this love language is expressed and received. What feels deeply loving to one person might feel insignificant or even misplaced to another. To truly connect with your partner, it's essential to uncover the kinds of acts that matter most to them.

There are four primary dialects of acts of service: **saving time**, **alleviating stress**, **instilling security**, and **conveying care**. Each reflects a different way of expressing and receiving love through action. By understanding which of these speak most clearly to your partner, you can ensure your efforts are not only noticed but deeply appreciated.

When done with thoughtfulness, acts of service become more than tasks—they become powerful gestures of love. In the following sections, we'll unpack these four dialects and explore how each can be tailored to show your partner just how much they mean to you.

ACTS OF SERVICE DIALECT #1

Saving Time

As the saying goes, "Time is the one thing we can never get back." For someone who values the saving time dialect of acts of service, that couldn't be more true. Acts that free up their time—like running errands, prepping a meal, or tackling chores—are seen as meaningful expressions of love.

This dialect isn't just about helping out; it's about recognizing the pressures of daily life and stepping in to create breathing room. By saving time for your partner, you're saying, "I see how much you have on your plate, and I want to make things easier for you."

For someone who values saving time, every minute you give back feels like a heartfelt gesture—a practical, loving way of showing that you truly care. It may not come naturally at first, but once you see how much it means to your partner, the strangeness begins to fade, and the love behind the action becomes crystal clear.

Is Saving Time Your Partner's Dialect?

Does your partner really appreciate it when you step in to help with tasks that make their day run more efficiently? Do they seem especially grateful when you take something off their plate, freeing up time for them to focus on what matters most? If they value efficiency and appreciate acts that give them more time, saving time is likely their primary acts of service dialect.

You know saving time is your partner's dialect if:

- ☐ They comment on how much they appreciate you helping with errands or daily tasks.
- ☐ They're quick to express gratitude when you complete a time-consuming chore for them, like cleaning the house or preparing a meal.
- ☐ They seem most relaxed and happy when their schedule feels more manageable because of your help.

- ☐ They frequently talk about feeling overwhelmed by their to-do list and value help in making it more manageable.
- ☐ They light up when you anticipate their needs, like picking up something they need without being asked.
- ☐ They express frustration when they feel like they're managing everything on their own.
- ☐ They often acknowledge how meaningful it is when you take initiative to save them time, even in small ways.

If this sounds like your partner, saving time is likely their primary dialect. For someone who values this approach, every action that gives them a little extra breathing room is a powerful way of saying, "I love you."

Eli knew that Autumn's love language was acts of service. And lately, he could tell she was running on fumes.

Since starting a hybrid job downtown—part remote, part in-person—her days had gotten longer and her to-do list never shorter. Between meetings, traffic, and managing life's moving parts, even small errands felt overwhelming.

One night over dinner, she mentioned needing to renew her passport before an upcoming work trip.

"I've got to find time to get to the post office this week," she said with a sigh. "But they close before I'm even done working. I might have to take time off."

Eli just nodded, tucked the thought away—and the next morning, left early.

He stood in line at the passport office for nearly an hour, filled out all the preliminary paperwork, and scheduled the soonest possible appointment. When Autumn came home, he handed her a small slip of paper and said, "You've got a five-minute appointment tomorrow at noon. Just bring your ID—they're expecting you."

Autumn stared at him. "You waited in line? You *did* this?"

He shrugged. "Figured I can't make your days less busy, but I can help you get some time back."

She looked at him with a mix of disbelief and deep gratitude. "That's honestly one of the most loving things you've ever done."

That's what the saving time dialect looks like. It's not flashy or poetic—but it speaks volumes. For Autumn, it said: *I know your time is valuable. Let me give some of it back to you.* And for Eli, that hour in line was love—lived out, not just said.

Why Saving Time Matters

This dialect speaks to one of the most fundamental human desires: the need to feel supported and understood in the face of life's endless demands. For someone who resonates with this dialect, acts that free up their time aren't just practical—they're deeply validating. They show your partner that you recognize their stress, value their priorities, and care enough to help lighten their load.

Psychologically, saving time acknowledges the mental and emotional weight that comes with a busy life. It's more than just ticking off tasks—it's about reducing cognitive overload and creating space for your partner to focus on what brings them joy or peace. These acts of service aren't simply gestures of love, they provide tangible relief, fostering a sense of partnership and shared responsibility that strengthens the emotional bond.

For someone who values saving time, these acts go beyond efficiency. They communicate empathy, care, and an understanding of their inner world. Saving Time tells your partner, "I'm here to help." It's a powerful way to show love in a world where time often feels like the most precious—and elusive—resource.

ACTS OF SERVICE DIALECT #2

Alleviating Stress

This dialect steps in to ease your partner's burdens and calm their worries. For someone who resonates with this dialect, acts that reduce stress—whether by solving a problem or handling an overwhelming task—speak volumes about your care and support.

It's about more than simply being helpful—it's about understanding what emotionally weighs on your partner and taking intentional action to lighten that load. Whether it's staying up late to help them meet a deadline, handling a long-overdue chore, or even taking the kids out of the house to give them a moment to breathe, these acts say, "You're not in this alone."

As Hans Selye, the pioneering stress researcher, once said, "It's not stress that kills us, it is our reaction to it." For someone who values this dialect, your acts of service help shift their experience from feeling overwhelmed to feeling supported, and from chaos to a sense of order. Alleviating Stress is a profound way to demonstrate love—not just in words but in actions that create peace amidst the demands of life.

Is Alleviating Stress Your Partner's Dialect?

Does your partner seem most at ease when you take action to help lighten their burdens? Do they feel especially loved when you step in to solve a problem, handle a task, or reduce the chaos in their life? If they value efforts that create calm, alleviating stress may be their primary acts of service dialect.

You know alleviating stress is your partner's dialect if:

- ☐ They often express gratitude when you take care of a task that's been weighing heavily on them.

- ☐ They seem visibly more relaxed when you step in to lend practical help during overwhelming moments.
- ☐ They appreciate when you notice their stress without being asked and take initiative to address it.
- ☐ They often mention how much they value your support in times of high pressure or emotional strain.
- ☐ They respond especially positively when you simplify their day, like prepping meals, handling the kids, or managing logistics during a busy week.
- ☐ They've shared that having you "take something off their plate" makes them feel deeply supported and cared for.
- ☐ They feel most loved when you show up not just in moments of joy, but also in times of challenge.

If this list resonates with your partner, alleviating stress is likely their primary dialect. For someone who values this approach, the best way to show love is to ease their burdens and help create the calm and balance they crave.

Jake and Eliza had been married for three years. Jake was burning the candle at both ends—working full-time while trying to finish his degree online. Deadlines, papers, Zoom meetings. He was constantly on edge.

More than once, he'd muttered, "I don't know if I can pull this off. I'm so stressed. Maybe I bit off more than I can chew."

Eliza, a nurse with a rotating hospital schedule, saw it all—the sleepless nights, the tension in his shoulders, the way he stopped laughing at his own jokes. She knew how much finishing his degree meant to him. And she knew he was running on fumes.

So one weekend, after a quiet breakfast, she gently placed her hand on his and said, "Babe, I see how hard you're pushing yourself. And I know this season is a lot. So I've made a few changes—I canceled the out-of-town trip we had planned, just to give you a breather. I also booked you a 90-minute massage next Saturday. No strings. Just time to reset."

Jake blinked. "Wait . . . what? Seriously?"

She nodded. "You don't have to power through everything alone. I want to help carry some of this stress with you. Because I believe in you. And I want you to finish strong."

Jake didn't say anything at first—he just pulled her into a long, grateful hug.

That's the stress-reducing dialect of acts of service. It's not about doing more—it's about easing the weight someone else is carrying. For Jake, Eliza's actions said: *You matter. Your mental health matters. And we're in this together.*

When you love someone under pressure, the most powerful gift you can give might be peace.

Why Alleviating Stress Matters

From a psychological perspective, stress triggers a cascade of physiological and emotional responses, often leading to a heightened state of anxiety or exhaustion. When you alleviate stress for your partner, you help reduce this burden, allowing them to return to a state of calm and focus.

For someone who values this dialect, alleviating stress also builds emotional safety. It shows that you're not just present in moments of ease but actively invested in their well-being when things get tough. Psychologist Shelley Taylor's concept of "tend and befriend" underscores how supportive gestures in times of stress deepen relational bonds, fostering resilience and connection.[17] Alleviating stress isn't just about solving problems—it's about nurturing a relationship that thrives in both calm and chaos.

ACTS OF SERVICE DIALECT #3

Instilling Security

Psychologist Sue Johnson notes that when we feel secure, we stop looking for reassurance and start focusing on the connection. This is true of everyone. But it's especially true of the person who speaks this dialect.

Acts of service that instill security provide consistency, dependability, and a sense of safety. And for the person who speaks this dialect, it's how they feel most loved. What does it look like? This could involve maintaining a steady routine of managing your finances, or taking proactive steps to ensure the household runs smoothly. It might also mean being their go-to in times of crisis, like handling unexpected repairs or stepping in to manage logistics when life feels chaotic. Even small acts, like always ensuring the pantry is stocked or keeping track of important dates or staying on top of doctor appointments, can make a significant impact.

It's about offering reliability through actions that show your partner they can count on you, no matter what. These gestures aren't necessarily grand, but they provide peace of mind and carry significant weight, as they build trust and create a foundation where love can flourish.

Is Instilling Security Your Partner's Dialect?

Does your partner feel most loved when you take actions that create stability and consistency in their life? Do they thrive on the comfort of knowing you're dependable and proactive? If they value gestures that provide emotional and practical reassurance, instilling security may be their primary acts of service dialect.

You know instilling security is your partner's dialect if:

- ☐ They express gratitude when you handle tasks that provide long-term stability, like budgeting, scheduling, or planning ahead.

- ☐ They feel reassured when you take care of practical details, such as maintaining the car, paying bills on time, or organizing the household.
- ☐ They seem most at ease when routines are consistent, and they don't have to worry about unpredictable disruptions.
- ☐ They often talk about how much they value knowing they can count on you in times of uncertainty or stress.
- ☐ They light up when you take initiative to address potential problems before they arise, such as scheduling repairs or anticipating future needs.
- ☐ They feel deeply cared for when you provide both emotional and logistical support, especially during challenging times.
- ☐ They frequently comment on how your actions make them feel safe, supported, and secure.

If this list resonates with your partner, instilling security is likely their primary dialect. For someone who values this approach, the love you show through dependable and stabilizing actions helps build a foundation of trust and peace that allows your relationship to thrive.

Daniel and Riley had been married just over five years. They loved each other deeply, but they were wired differently. Riley was spontaneous, creative, and warm. Daniel was steady, thoughtful, and practical—sometimes to the point of seeming predictable.

At first, Riley didn't fully notice the small things Daniel did week after week.

He always filled her gas tank on Sundays. He checked their bank accounts every Friday and made sure all the bills were paid by the end of the day. When her car registration was due, he had it renewed before she even got the reminder in the mail.

She used to tease him: "You and your routines."

But over time, she realized something deeper—those routines weren't just habits. They were love.

One night, they were sitting on the couch when Riley said quietly, "You know what I've been thinking about lately?"

Daniel looked up from his laptop. "What's that?"

"I never have to worry about things falling apart. Not with you. You don't just say you've got my back—you show it, every single day. It makes me feel . . . safe. Like I can exhale."

Daniel smiled, a little surprised. "I guess that's how I love you best. By keeping things steady."

That's the security dialect within acts of service. It's not flashy or loud. It's consistent. Quiet. Reliable. It says, *You're safe here. I've got us.*

For Riley, it became the rhythm she didn't know her soul needed—until she saw it for what it was: love in the form of stability.

Why Security Matters

Psychologically, when we feel secure, we can fully invest in our relationships without being consumed by fear or instability. For someone who values this dialect of acts of service, security provides the emotional and practical reassurance they need to open their heart and trust deeply. As Scottish poet and minister George MacDonald is credited with saying, "To be trusted is a greater compliment than being loved."

Stress and uncertainty activate the brain's threat response, often leaving people emotionally depleted and disconnected. By creating a sense of security through dependable actions, you help calm this response, making room for deeper emotional intimacy. Security fosters trust, and trust is the bedrock of any strong, loving relationship.

For someone who values security, it's not just about the immediate relief your actions bring—it's about the long-term message they convey: "I'm here for you, no matter what." This reassurance allows them to focus less on potential fears or anxieties and more on building a life with you, one rooted in trust, safety, and love.

ACTS OF SERVICE DIALECT #4

Conveying Care

The power of your actions in this dialect lies in intentionality—small, meaningful gestures that say, "I'm thinking of you, and I want to make your day better." As Theodore Roosevelt is attributed with saying, "People don't care how much you know until they know how much you care." This dialect embodies that truth by showing love not through words but through thoughtful actions that speak directly to your partner's heart.

Conveying care through acts of service might mean warming up their car on a cold morning, remembering to restock their favorite snack, or organizing a space they've been too overwhelmed to tackle. It could look like surprising them with a small, meaningful treat after a long day or thoughtfully charging their devices before a trip because you know they'd forget. What matters isn't the size of the action but the intentionality behind it—these gestures reflect love in its most practical and heartfelt form.

Conveying care bridges the gap between thought and action, turning affection into something tangible. These simple but impactful acts demonstrate not just your love, but your willingness to show up in the everyday details of life. They create a powerful connection rooted in trust, thoughtfulness, and an ongoing sense that you're in tune with what truly matters to your partner.

Is Conveying Care Your Partner's Dialect?

Does your partner seem most touched by gestures that reflect you've noticed their needs and acted on them? If they value these little moments of intentionality, conveying care may be their primary acts of service dialect.

You know conveying care is your partner's dialect if:

- ☐ They appreciate when you surprise them with small comforts, like their favorite snack or a warm drink after a long day.
- ☐ They notice and comment on how meaningful it is when you take care of something for them without being asked.
- ☐ They feel seen and loved when you remember their preferences, like how they take their coffee or their favorite brand of toothpaste.
- ☐ They often express gratitude for acts that reflect forethought, such as packing something they forgot or setting out an umbrella on a rainy day.
- ☐ They light up when you do something thoughtful that they didn't expect, like charging their phone overnight.
- ☐ They feel most cared for by the little things, especially when they reflect that you're paying attention to the details of their life.
- ☐ They feel especially loved when you step in to help with parenting responsibilities, like getting the kids ready for school or managing bedtime when they're feeling overwhelmed.

If this sounds like your partner, conveying care is likely their primary dialect. For someone who values this approach, small actions aren't just practical—they're deeply personal reminders that they are loved, seen, and treasured.

Nico had always been the strong one—steady, capable, rarely asking for help. But after catching a nasty flu that knocked him out for days, he was forced to slow down. His wife, Jordan, stepped in without hesitation. But it wasn't just what she did—it was *how* she did it.

She didn't just bring him soup. She checked the temperature so it wouldn't burn his throat. She didn't just grab meds from the pharmacy. She picked up his favorite electrolyte drink and tucked a handwritten note inside the bag. She didn't hover, but she noticed. She noticed when he got too quiet. When he needed a fresh shirt. When he was tired of being stuck in bed and needed a little company.

One night, as she was fluffing his pillow and setting a cool washcloth on his forehead, Nico whispered, "You're kind of amazing, you know that?"

Jordan smiled. "You take care of everyone else all the time. Let me take care of you for a while."

That's the care dialect of acts of service. It's not just about *doing* things—it's about *tending* to someone. *I notice you. I'm here for you. You don't have to ask.*

For Nico, who was used to pushing through and powering on, Jordan's quiet caregiving was deeply disarming—and felt deeply loving.

Why Care Matters

Small acts of care activate what social psychologists call the "supportive presence." This is the feeling of knowing someone is not only aware of your needs but also willing to act on them in ways that prioritize your well-being. These actions foster trust and deepen emotional intimacy, strengthening the bond between you and your partner.

Caring gestures reduce cognitive and emotional load. When a partner steps in to handle a task or anticipates a need, it alleviates mental strain and creates space for joy, relaxation, or connection. This is particularly impactful in relationships, as studies show that perceived partner responsiveness—the sense that your partner "gets you"—is a cornerstone of long-term relational satisfaction.

For someone who values this dialect, small acts of love create a powerful message: "You are worth my time, my energy, and my attention." Care matters because it turns the ordinary into the extraordinary, making daily life feel just a little more meaningful and deeply connected.

We've explored the four primary dialects of acts of service: saving time, alleviating stress, instilling security, and conveying care. These four capture the essence of what truly matters when it comes to serving your partner. Your partner may appreciate all of them, of course, but they're likely to have one that continually tops the list.

However, you can overdo acts of service, leading to an overload that not healthy or helpful for anyone.

Avoiding Acts of Service Overload

If you're constantly stepping in to handle every little thing—organizing their sock drawer, packing their lunch, or buying a new paint color for the bathroom without their input—your partner might start feeling less loved and more micromanaged. For someone who values acts of service, it's not about doing *everything* for them—it's about doing the right things that truly make a difference.

To avoid overload, focus on the tasks that matter most to your partner. Thoughtful gestures—like taking care of a stressful chore they've been dreading—speak volumes, whereas going overboard with unnecessary help might feel more like overstepping. Nobody wants to come home and discover you've reorganized their kitchen cabinets "for efficiency" without being asked.

It's also important to remember that love isn't about keeping score. If your partner starts feeling like every gesture comes with a tally sheet or a subtle "Did you notice what I did for you?" vibe, it might be time to scale back. By offering acts of service that are intentional and meaningful, you'll ensure your efforts feel like love—not an unsolicited performance review.

Acts of service can sometimes feel more labor-intensive than other love languages. But in reality, acts of service isn't about exhausting efforts. It's not about turning into your partner's personal assistant or taking on every chore in sight.

At its heart, acts of service is about love in action—seeing what your partner needs and meeting them in ways that lighten their load and brighten their day. Thoughtful acts, where you set your own agenda aside for a moment to meet theirs, speak louder than words ever could for someone whose love language is service.

So, while Seth Meyers may have exaggerated the "workload" of acts of service, he wasn't wrong about one thing: It requires effort. But here's the truth—it's effort worth giving. Because when your partner feels cared for, supported, and loved in ways that matter most to them, it builds an incredible connection between you. And that is worth every bit of "sweat equity."

TAKE THE NEXT STEP

Discovering your partner's specific dialect of acts of service can help you show love in ways that truly matter to them. Do they feel most supported when you save time, alleviate stress, instill security, or convey care through your actions?

The 5 Love Languages Premium Assessment is designed to uncover these unique preferences, providing personalized insights into the acts that resonate most deeply with your partner. It's a practical tool to ensure that your efforts feel thoughtful, meaningful, and deeply appreciated.

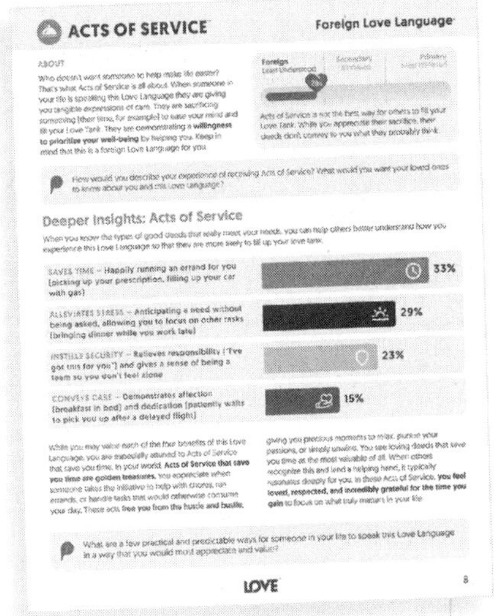

Take the Premium Assessment today and discover how to speak acts of service in a way that strengthens your connection and lightens your partner's load.

5LoveLanguages.com/Premium

CHAPTER 11

Physical Touch

Saying Everything Without Speaking a Word

Physical touch has never been the primary love language for either of us (Les and Leslie), but that doesn't mean it hasn't had a profound impact on our lives. In fact, we learned about the power of touch in one of the most vulnerable moments of our journey together: the birth of our first baby, John.

Born three months premature and weighing only one pound, John spent his first several months in an isolette in the NICU of a Seattle hospital. Machines hummed and beeped around him as we sat by his side in sterile gowns, watching his tiny chest rise and fall. For ten long days, we hadn't been able to hold him—his fragile body couldn't tolerate the stimulation of touch.

But on February 18, his nurse, Margaret, quietly asked if I'd like to hold John in my arms. I (Leslie) immediately teared up. It wasn't just a milestone for John—it was my birthday. And it turned out to be the best gift I've ever received.

Margaret wrapped him in blankets warmed in the oven, carefully bundled him with tubes and wires still attached, and placed him in my arms. I held him for just ten minutes, but those ten minutes felt like a turning point—not only for me but for him.

The next day, as John lay in his isolette, we were allowed to reach through its portals to gently hold him with one hand on his head and the other around his tiny feet. Soon after, his doctors introduced us to "kangaroo care," the practice of holding a preemie skin-to-skin against your chest. It was life-giving for John and transformative for us.

As John grew, we realized just how vital touch had been to his development and to our bond as parents. We dove into the research, learning that human touch has profound benefits—not just for premature babies but for everyone. Anthropologist Helen Fisher describes this beautifully in *Anatomy of Love*: "Human skin is like a field of grass, each blade a nerve ending so sensitive that the slightest graze can etch into the human brain a memory of the moment."[18]

A simple touch—a squeeze on the shoulder, a soft graze on the arm—can express what words sometimes can't: "I'm here," "I see you," "I love you." For those whose love language is physical touch, these gestures aren't fleeting—they're foundational.

If touch is your partner's love language, you probably already know how much it means to them. Chapter 8 in *The 5 Love Languages* gives an overview of how love is expressed through physical touch. But what you may not realize is that there are many "dialects" of touch—unique ways it can be expressed. Later in this chapter, we'll explore seven distinct types of touch and help you discover which ones resonate most deeply with your partner. Because at its core, physical touch is more than a fleeting gesture—it's a love letter written in the language of skin-on-skin.

A Quick Review

Physical touch is about connection through closeness. It's not just about intimacy—it's about the comfort, security, and love communicated through physical presence and contact. For someone whose heart resonates with this love language, touch is a powerful way to feel loved, supported, and connected.

Ways to Practice **Physical Touch**

- *Holding hands while walking together, even during the simplest errands.*
- *Giving them a long hug when they've had a tough day.*
- *Sitting close on the couch and resting your hand on their arm or shoulder.*
- *Offering a gentle back rub or head massage while you're relaxing together.*
- *Playfully brushing their hair out of their face or squeezing their hand for reassurance.*

For those who thrive on physical touch, it's not about grand romantic gestures—it's about consistent, thoughtful touches that remind them of your care and affection.

As we delve into this love language, you'll discover ways to be attuned to your partner's comfort and preferences, finding meaningful ways to show love through touch that speaks directly to their heart.

Why Physical Touch Speaks Straight to the Heart

Physical touch meets a deep human need for connection and comfort. While everyone benefits from touch in some way, for some, physical contact resonates on a deeper emotional level. Our early experiences with touch—whether nurturing or neglectful—shape how we associate physical closeness with love and security. Whether it's filling a void left by a lack of affectionate touch or reinforcing a solid foundation of safety, physical touch communicates care in a way that words often cannot.

Psychologically, individuals drawn to this love language are deeply attuned to nonverbal cues. Research on how we bond suggests that touch plays a critical role in forming emotional connections during infancy and childhood. Those who lacked physical affection growing up may crave it to overcome feelings of detachment or insecurity, while those who received consistent, loving touch often associate it with stability and connection in relationships.

From a sensory perspective, touch stimulates the release of oxytocin, often called the "bonding hormone," which fosters trust, relaxation, and emotional closeness. For individuals with this love language, the warmth of a handhold or the reassurance of a hug isn't just nice—it's essential to their emotional well-being.

Personality traits can also amplify the significance of touch. For example, warm and emotionally expressive individuals may find physical touch to be the most natural way to give and receive love. Similarly, those with heightened sensitivity may interpret even small gestures—like a pat on the back or a brush of the hand—as profound acts of affection.

In essence, for someone who thrives on physical touch, it's not just about proximity; it's about the reassurance and intimacy conveyed through it. A simple touch can bridge emotional gaps, offer solace, and speak love in a way words never could.

When Physical Touch Matters Most

Physical touch is a universal language of love, but for someone whose primary love language is touch, there are certain moments when it becomes especially powerful.

Times of Emotional Upset

Moments of sadness, frustration, or fear often call for the reassuring presence of a warm embrace or a gentle touch. Maybe they're simply feeling defeated after a stressful workday or overwhelmed by bad news.

For example, when they're feeling overwhelmed after a hard day, wrapping them in a tight, grounding hug without saying anything at all can help them feel safe and understood. Physical touch during these moments isn't about solving their problems but about offering solace.

Times of Joy

Celebratory moments—whether it's a big win, a cherished milestone, or even a small but meaningful victory—are the perfect times for physical touches that amplify excitement and pride. A triumphant high-five, a playful squeeze, or a celebratory kiss can turn their joy into something even bigger, showing that their happiness is yours too.

For example, grabbing their hand and spinning them into a spontaneous twirl after hearing great news or an affectionate forehead kiss says, "I'm bursting with pride for you." These heartfelt gestures add spark and intimacy, making the moment even more unforgettable.

Times of Distance

Physical touch becomes essential during moments of emotional distance. These are times when busyness, stress, or conflict might make them feel disconnected from you. A gentle, nonverbal touch can break through the tension and remind them of your bond, even when words fail.

For example, reaching for their hand while sitting together on the couch or placing a comforting hand on their back during a tough conversation can say, "I'm still here with you, and we're in this together."

When Not to Focus on Physical Touch

Touch should always feel respectful, appropriate, and welcomed—offering it at the wrong time or in the wrong way can diminish its impact or even create tension. For example, avoid physical touch when your partner is visibly upset and tensions are high. In these situations, resolving the conflict first can make touch feel more authentic and reassuring later.

Heightened emotions often need space, not touch. A well-meaning hug, a pat on the back, or a hand on their shoulder might feel like an attempt to brush aside their emotions rather than offer genuine support. Instead, wait for cues that they are ready for connection, or ask with all sincerity and warmth, "Would you like a hug?" to ensure your gesture will be received positively.

Another time to be cautious is during conflict. Reaching out physically—such as trying to hold their hand or embrace them—when tensions are still high might come across as dismissive or a way to avoid addressing the real issue.

It's also important to be mindful of public settings. Some people may feel uncomfortable with displays of affection in front of others, even if they usually enjoy physical touch in private. Respecting their boundaries in these moments ensures that your gesture will be received positively.

Lastly, consider your own intention. If the touch carries an unspoken expectation—such as initiating affection with the hope of something in return—it can feel like a quid pro quo exchange rather than a genuinely loving gesture. Physical touch should be about offering connection, not seeking a reward.

How Physical Touch Can Get Lost in Translation

Physical affection can miss the mark when your partner isn't in the mood for it. For example, swooping in for a big hug while they're frantically trying to meet a work deadline might feel less like a sweet moment and more like you're getting between them and their sanity. Timing is crucial—if they're stressed or focused, your well-meaning gesture might just come across as irritating. Touch works best when it meets *their* needs, not just your craving for a cuddle.

It's also important to respect personal preferences and boundaries. Sure, a playful poke or tickle might seem like harmless fun to you, but if your partner doesn't enjoy it, then it will more likely come across as annoying than affectionate. Understanding what types of touch they actually appreciate—and when—is the difference between making them smile and making their eyes roll.

Finally, physical touch can lose its meaning when it doesn't match the emotional tone of the moment. For example, giving your partner a quick peck on the cheek right after snapping, "Why can't you ever load the dishwasher right?" might feel less like affection and more like a confusing plot twist. In moments like this, your partner is probably thinking, "What just happened?" For touch to truly connect, it needs to feel authentic and in sync with your partner's feelings.

And of course, there's one more way physical touch can miss the mark: when you don't recognize the nuances of your partner's preferences—like a love for cuddles but a hatred of sweaty hand-holding. That's a discussion worth having.

Discovering the Dialects of Physical Touch

Like the other four love languages, physical touch comes with its own unique dialects—specific ways that this love language can be expressed and experienced. Not all forms of touch carry the same meaning, and what feels loving and meaningful to one person might not resonate as much with another. To truly connect with your partner, it's important to uncover the kinds of touch that speak most deeply to them.

There are seven primary dialects of physical touch. That's right, seven! **Comfort**, **affection**, **playfulness**, **romance**, **protection**, **expression**, and **restoration.** It's practically a love language buffet. Each one represents a distinct way of using touch to convey love and create connection. Understanding which of these resonates most with your partner is like having a personalized code to their heart.

In the sections ahead, we'll explore these seven dialects, unpacking how each one uniquely contributes to the powerful language of touch. Together, they form a rich vocabulary for building closeness and communicating love in ways that words often cannot.

PHYSICAL TOUCH DIALECT #1

Comforting Touch

Comforting touch is all about providing reassurance, safety, and care through physical connection. For someone who resonates with this dialect, touch becomes a source of emotional stability during times of stress, sadness, or uncertainty. A gentle hug, holding hands during a difficult moment, or simply placing a hand on their shoulder can convey, "I'm here for you," in ways that words cannot. This kind of touch is less about affection and more about offering support and grounding.

Is Comforting Touch Your Partner's Dialect?

Does your partner instinctively reach for your hand during emotional moments or relax noticeably when you offer a comforting hug? Do they seem most soothed by physical connection in times of stress? You know comforting touch is your partner's dialect if:

- ☐ They often seek physical closeness when feeling stressed, sad, or overwhelmed.

- ☐ They seem comforted by small gestures, like a hand on their back or an arm around their shoulders.
- ☐ They feel reassured when you offer a touch during difficult conversations or emotional challenges.
- ☐ They frequently comment on how much physical presence helps them feel grounded and secure.

If this sounds like your partner, comforting touch is likely how they feel most loved and supported.

Sam didn't need words—he just needed to be held. After a rough day at work, he walked in, dropped his bag, and collapsed onto the couch. His shoulders were tight. His jaw clenched. Something was clearly off, but he wasn't ready to talk.

Emily didn't ask questions. She just sat beside him, leaned in, and wrapped her arms around him. One hand on his back, the other gently holding his.

They stayed like that—no words, no pressure, just presence.

Eventually, Sam let out a deep sigh and said, "Thanks. I didn't even realize how much I needed that."

That's the comfort dialect of physical touch. Not passionate or playful—but grounding. A quiet hug. A steady hand. A touch that says, *I'm here with you.*

For Sam, it was exactly the kind of love his body understood best.

Why Comfort Matters

From infancy, physical touch is how we are soothed and reassured, and that need doesn't disappear with age. Comforting touch calms the nervous system, reducing stress hormones and fostering emotional security. It communicates that you are a safe harbor in the storms of life. It says, "I'm with you," not just in words but in the tangible presence of your touch.

PHYSICAL TOUCH DIALECT #2

Affectionate Touch

This is the physical expression of fondness and warmth. It's about playful kisses, casual hugs, holding hands, or cuddling on the couch. This kind of touch is spontaneous and lighthearted, often happening during everyday moments. It's not tied to moments of stress or passion but simply about expressing affection in the little rhythms of life together. Affectionate touch creates a sense of closeness that strengthens your bond daily.

Is Affectionate Touch Your Partner's Dialect?

Does your partner naturally gravitate toward you for hugs, kisses, or other casual physical contact? Do they light up when you reach for their hand or put your arm around them? You know affectionate touch is your partner's dialect if:

- ☐ They frequently initiate casual touch, like leaning on you, resting their hand on your leg, or brushing your arm.
- ☐ They seem happiest when physical affection is part of your everyday interactions.
- ☐ They often comment on how much they love simple gestures, like hugs or holding hands.
- ☐ They seem especially reassured by small, affectionate touches during the day, even without a specific reason.

If this sounds like your partner, affectionate touch is likely how they feel most connected and cherished.

Lena didn't need grand gestures—she needed connection. She and Marcus had been married almost a decade, and while life was full—kids, work, errands—she sometimes felt like they were just passing each other in the hallway.

One Saturday morning, while making coffee, Marcus walked up behind her and wrapped his arms around her waist. He kissed her shoulder and rested his chin on her neck.

She melted.

He didn't say anything, and he didn't need to. That warm, familiar touch told her everything: *I see you. I still choose you.*

That's the affection dialect of physical touch. A hand on the back. Fingers laced while watching TV. A kiss on the forehead in the kitchen. It says, *We're still us.*

For Lena, it wasn't about heat or healing—it was about staying close in the everyday.

Why Affection Matters

Affection keeps the spark of connection alive in the everyday flow of life. Consistent physical affection releases oxytocin, the "bonding hormone," which fosters trust and intimacy in relationships. Affectionate Touch is a way of saying, "I love you," without words. It bridges emotional distance, reinforces closeness, and builds a foundation of warmth and care. For someone who values this dialect, these small, spontaneous gestures of affection are the heartbeat of a loving relationship.

PHYSICAL TOUCH DIALECT #3

Playful Touch

This brings a sense of lightness and fun into your relationship. It's about tickling, teasing pokes, playful nudges, or even a quick pillow fight.

For someone who resonates with this dialect, touch isn't just a way to connect—it's a way to spark joy and laughter in your relationship. This type of touch is carefree and energetic, adding a sense of spontaneity to your connection. It's not about deep emotional support or romantic gestures—it's about keeping things light, fun, and engaging.

Is Playful Touch Your Partner's Dialect?

Does your partner thrive on physical interactions that make them laugh or smile? Do they enjoy teasing touches or playful moments of physical connection? You know playful touch is your partner's dialect if:

- ☐ They love jokingly tapping or nudging you to grab your attention.
- ☐ They frequently initiate playful physical gestures, like tickling or light wrestling.
- ☐ They often laugh or smile when physical playfulness is part of your interactions.
- ☐ They seem to use playful touch to defuse tension or lighten the mood during stressful moments.

If this sounds like your partner, playful touch is likely how they feel most connected and energized in your relationship.

Evan and Talia didn't take themselves too seriously. Even during stressful weeks, they found little ways to keep things light. For Talia, that often meant playful touch.

One night, as Evan passed by in the hallway, she flicked him with a dish towel and took off running. He laughed, chased her into the living room, and tackled her gently onto the couch.

They were both laughing, breathless and smiling, wrapped up in the kind of silly, spontaneous moment that reminded them why they worked so well together.

That's the playfulness dialect of physical touch. A quick shoulder bump, an unexpected tickle, a mock wrestling match on the bed. It says, *We still know how to have fun—together.*

For Talia, it wasn't about intensity or comfort—it was about joy, surprise, and staying connected through laughter.

Why Playfulness Matters

Playfulness breaks up the seriousness of daily life. It builds emotional resilience and reinforces a sense of shared happiness. Playful touch reminds you not to take life—or each other—too seriously. For someone who values this dialect, these gestures are about more than just fun, they create a lighthearted connection that strengthens your bond and keeps your relationship vibrant and engaging.

PHYSICAL TOUCH DIALECT #4

Romantic Touch

Romantic touch is all about igniting intimacy and desire. It's the kind of touch that lingers—a handhold during a quiet moment, a kiss that says more than words ever could, or the gentle brush of your partner's face that sends a shiver straight to their heart. It's the spark that keeps romance alive, adding layers of thoughtfulness and tenderness to your connection. Romantic touch wraps your relationship in intimacy, making even the simplest moments feel like something extraordinary.

Is Romantic Touch Your Partner's Dialect?

Does your partner cherish physical gestures that evoke a sense of love and intimacy? Do they light up when touch feels meaningful and deliberate, like holding hands with special squeezes or a slow embrace and a lingering kiss? You know romantic touch is your partner's dialect if:

- ☐ They savor meaningful touches, like holding hands during a quiet conversation or cuddling during a movie.
- ☐ They appreciate slow, intentional gestures, like a lingering kiss or a gentle caress.
- ☐ They often talk about how much they value physical connection that feels purposeful and loving.
- ☐ They seem most fulfilled when physical touch enhances the emotional atmosphere of a moment, like a kiss under the stars or a hug after a heartfelt conversation.

If this sounds like your partner, romantic touch is likely how they feel most cherished and emotionally connected.

Noah had always been affectionate, but what made Emma feel most loved was touch that felt intentional—romantic, not routine.

One Friday night, he lit a few candles in the living room, queued up their favorite slow songs, and reached for her hand.

"Dance with me?" he asked.

She smiled and stepped into his arms. As they swayed together, his hand traced the small of her back, and he whispered, "You're still the most beautiful part of my world."

That's the romance dialect of physical touch. It's not about passion or play—it's about tenderness with intention. A soft kiss on the hand. A lingering embrace. A touch that says, *You still take my breath away.*

For Emma, it wasn't about quantity—it was about *how* the touch was given: thoughtfully, lovingly, and from the heart.

Why Romance Matters

Romantic touch floods the body with oxytocin that deepens trust and strengthens closeness. But its magic goes beyond chemistry.

Romantic touch weaves together emotional and physical connection, transforming ordinary moments into something unforgettable. It's not just about the act of touching, it's about crafting an atmosphere of tenderness and devotion that whispers, "You're my one, and I choose you every day." This kind of touch keeps love alive and electric, nurturing the deep, soulful bond every relationship needs to flourish.

PHYSICAL TOUCH DIALECT #5

Protective Touch

Protective touch is about offering safety, reassurance, and a sense of security through physical connection. This type of touch communicates, "I've got you," in moments of uncertainty or danger. Whether it's pulling your partner close during a crowded event, wrapping them in a warm embrace during a storm, or instinctively reaching for their hand when they feel uneasy, protective touch is a physical promise of care and protection.

Is Protective Touch Your Partner's Dialect?

Does your partner lean into your protective presence during moments of discomfort or uncertainty? You know protective touch is your partner's dialect if:

- ☐ They instinctively relax when you hold them close during moments of fear or tension.
- ☐ They feel reassured when you reach for their hand in crowded or overwhelming situations.
- ☐ They often seek physical comfort when feeling vulnerable, like leaning against you or holding on to you.
- ☐ They've expressed how much it means to them when you physically "shield" or stand close in moments of discomfort.

If this resonates, protective touch is likely how your partner feels most secure and cared for.

Kayla didn't always say when she felt anxious—but Liam could tell.

Crowds made her uneasy, especially in unfamiliar places. One evening at a packed concert, she started to tense. Without a word, Liam moved closer, placed his hand gently on her lower back, and kept it there as they navigated through the crowd.

She didn't say thank you. She didn't need to. She just exhaled—and relaxed into the space he made for her.

That's the protective dialect of physical touch. It's a guiding hand through a busy street. An arm around the shoulder when things feel uncertain. A physical reminder: *You're not alone. I've got you.*

For Kayla, that steady presence was more than comfort—it was security in skin and bone.

Why Protection Matters

This dialect satisfies the primal human need for safety. From an evolutionary perspective, physical connection has always been a way to signal security and solidarity in the face of uncertainty. Protective touch strengthens this instinct, reassuring your partner that you're there to guard and support them when life feels overwhelming. For someone who values this dialect, protective touch is love in its most instinctive form—a physical reminder that they are never alone and always protected.

PHYSICAL TOUCH DIALECT #6

Expressive Touch

Expressive touch is all about using physical connection to convey a wide range of emotions—joy, excitement, congratulations, or even playful mischief. For someone who resonates with this dialect, touch becomes a dynamic form of communication, expressing feelings that words often can't capture. A celebratory high-five, a supportive squeeze of the hand, or an exuberant hug all fall into this category. This type of touch thrives on spontaneity and authenticity. It's about using physical gestures to share in your partner's emotional experience, creating a deeper sense of connection and understanding.

Is Expressive Touch Your Partner's Dialect?

Does your partner naturally use physical gestures to express their emotions, like reaching for a hug when they're happy or placing a hand on your shoulder to comfort you? You know expressive touch is your partner's dialect if:

- ☐ They often use touch to express a wide range of emotions, like joy, concern, or sympathy.
- ☐ They instinctively hug, pat, or hold you during emotionally charged moments.
- ☐ They respond enthusiastically to physical expressions of shared happiness, like a fist bump or playful nudge.
- ☐ They've expressed how much it means to them when you respond to their emotions with touch rather than just words.

If this resonates, expressive touch is likely how your partner feels most emotionally connected.

Judy was all energy and enthusiasm. She hugged friends before they even sat down, gave fist bumps after someone parallel parked, and greeted good news with a high five and a kiss on the cheek. Celebration wasn't optional—it was part of her personality. And for Judy, touch was how she expressed it.

Bruce, her husband, was more reserved. When she wrapped him in a full-body hug after his job promotion, he stood frozen, unsure how to respond. He hadn't realized she was speaking love in the way that came most naturally to her.

Then Bruce read *The 5 Love Languages*, and everything started to click. Judy wasn't just touchy—she was expressive. Her physical affection wasn't random—it was intentional, joyful, and deeply relational.

So Bruce started leaning in. He initiated high fives, welcomed spontaneous hugs, and even added a little flair to his greetings. Judy lit up. She felt seen, celebrated, and adored.

That's the expressiveness dialect of physical touch. It's animated, upbeat, and outward. A burst of affection that says, *I love you—and I love loving you.*

And for Judy, it was exactly the kind of touch that made her come alive.

Why Expressiveness Matters

This dialect transcends the limits of language, creating a direct and visceral connection between partners. Psychologically, physical gestures of expression tap into the part of our brain that manages emotions, making touch one of the most immediate and powerful ways to communicate feelings. For someone who values this dialect, expressive touch fosters a sense of emotional alignment and shared experience. It shows that you're not just observing their feelings but actively participating in them. Expressive touch brings you closer by speaking the language of emotions—without saying a single word.

PHYSICAL TOUCH DIALECT #7

Restorative Touch

This is all about renewal and healing. It's the kind of touch that soothes, relaxes, and helps your partner recharge physically and emotionally. For someone who resonates with this dialect, touch becomes a balm for stress, tension, or exhaustion—whether it's a shoulder massage, a gentle back rub, or simply resting your hand on theirs while they unwind. This type of touch focuses on creating a calming, nurturing environment where your partner can feel safe and supported as they recover from the demands of life.

Is Restorative Touch Your Partner's Dialect?

Does your partner seem most relaxed and at ease when you offer soothing, comforting touch? You know restorative touch is your partner's dialect if:

- ☐ They frequently ask for or deeply appreciate massages, back rubs, or other soothing touch.
- ☐ They seem noticeably calmer and more relaxed after physical gestures of comfort.
- ☐ They often express how much they value physical touch as a way to de-stress or unwind.
- ☐ They gravitate toward physical connection when they're emotionally or physically drained.

If this resonates, restorative touch is likely how your partner feels most nurtured and renewed.

When Roger came home from work, he was often drained—emotionally and physically. On evenings when Michelle offered to give him a massage, he never turned her down. Her caring touch seemed to restore him, giving him the energy to enjoy the rest of the evening. What Michelle didn't realize was that she was speaking his love language—physical touch—in the dialect most meaningful to him. She hadn't read *The 5 Love Languages*, nor had Roger, but she had instinctively discovered what made him feel loved.

In turn, Roger often spoke Michelle's love language—words of affirmation. He regularly told her how beautiful she was and how much he loved her. "I'm so glad I married you," he'd say. "You're amazing."

Neither of them knew the concept of love languages, but somehow, they were both meeting each other's deepest emotional need for love.

Why Restoration Matters

Restorative touch activates a part of the body's nervous system that promotes relaxation and reduces stress hormones (like cortisol). This makes it one of the most powerful ways to help your partner regain a sense of balance and well-being. For someone who values this dialect, restorative touch isn't just about relaxation—it's about being cared for in a way that rejuvenates their mind, body, and spirit. It conveys a message of love through the simplest, most nurturing gestures, reminding them that you're not just present in their life—you're invested in their renewal and happiness.

Whew! That's seven potential dialects for physical touch. It's a lot, we know. And in all likelihood, your partner gravitates to all of them at some level. But it can be helpful to think of how they might prioritize them. Which one is at the top of their list? The bottom? The 5 Love Languages Premium Assessment can help with that.

The beauty of exploring all of these seven dialects is that it helps you focus on what truly matters to your partner, making your gestures of love more intentional and impactful. Whether it's the soothing comfort of restorative touch, the lightheartedness of playfulness, or the intimacy of romance, the key is paying attention to what resonates with your partner and embracing touch as a powerful language of connection.

But don't overdo it. Did you know that's possible? It is and it leads to touch-overload.

Avoiding Physical Touch Overload

In the early stages of a relationship, it's pretty normal to feel like you can't keep your hands off each other—it's all sparks, butterflies, and hand-holding marathons. But as time goes on, the constant touch can start to feel less romantic and more like being permanently glued together. For someone who values physical touch, it's not about *always* being in contact—it's about the kind of touch that feels meaningful and welcomed.

To avoid overload, be mindful of timing and context. A thoughtful hug when they've had a tough day or holding hands during a quiet moment can mean so much more than an endless stream of pats, pokes, or arm grabs. Nobody wants to feel like they're being pawed at when they're trying to load the dishwasher.

It's also worth checking in on your partner's boundaries and preferences. Just because *you're* in the mood for some physical affection doesn't mean they are—especially if they're tired or just need a little personal space. Touch should feel like love, not like you're auditioning to be their permanent shadow.

By being thoughtful and intentional with physical touch, you'll ensure it remains a source of connection and comfort rather than a running joke about how they can't make a move without you reaching out. Sometimes, less is more—and that makes the moments you do connect even sweeter.

We opened the chapter with the story of our baby John and how the power of touch became critical for his survival. That experience taught us something profound: touch isn't just physical—it's emotional, relational, and deeply human. It reaches beyond the surface, speaking a language of care, trust, and belonging. For those whose love language is physical touch, these moments are life-giving. They convey connection, comfort, and love in ways that words or actions alone often can't.

Touch is presence made tangible. It's the steady hand that says, "I'm here," the embrace that whispers, "You are safe," the gentle touch that reminds, "You are loved." In its simplest form, touch reassures us that we're not alone. Whether it's soothing a tiny newborn or quietly reassuring your partner with a handhold in the dark, touch has a way of bridging hearts.

But perhaps the most remarkable thing about touch is its humility. It doesn't demand attention or recognition. Its power lies in its quiet, everyday presence. It's the small moments—a brush on the arm, a kiss on the forehead, a hug after a long day—that speak the loudest. Touch is not extravagant, but it is essential, reminding us of the profound simplicity of human connection. It's a love letter, written one moment at a time, on the canvas of our partner's skin.

TAKE THE NEXT STEP

Uncovering your partner's specific dialect of physical touch can deepen your connection and make every gesture more meaningful. Do they feel most loved through comfort, affection, playfulness, romance, protection, expression, or restoration? **The 5 Love Languages Premium Assessment** helps you identify these unique preferences, offering personalized insights into the kinds of touch that speak love most powerfully to your partner. It's a simple way to ensure that your physical expressions of love truly resonate.

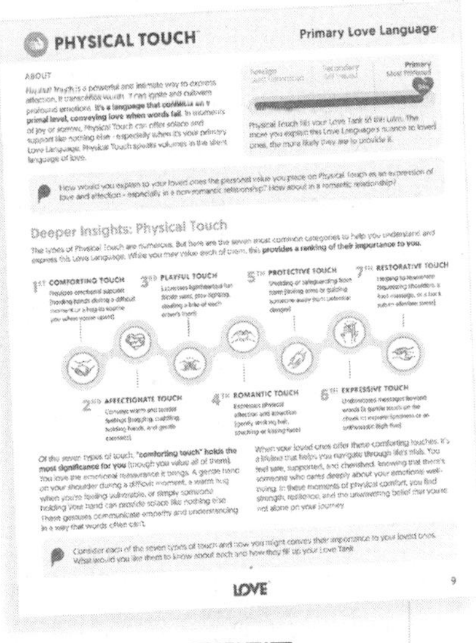

Take the Premium Assessment today and learn how to connect through physical touch in a way that brings warmth, closeness, and understanding to your relationship.

5LoveLanguages.com/Premium

Conclusion

Becoming a Love Language Virtuoso

Itzhak Perlman shuffled onto the stage at New York's Carnegie Hall, his crutches clicking against the polished floor. The iconic venue was packed to capacity, every seat filled with people who had come to witness not just a performance but a moment of musical transcendence. Each step Perlman took while carrying his beloved Stradivarius was deliberate, a triumph over the polio that had ravaged his body as a child but never claimed his spirit.

The audience held its collective breath as he reached center stage, carefully positioning himself in a chair set before the orchestra. There, under the glowing warmth of the stage lights, Perlman cradled his violin—the instrument that had been his voice, his passion, and his companion through decades of relentless practice. With the fluid precision of someone who had rehearsed this moment countless times, he raised the bow, resting it gently on the strings.

What followed was nothing short of magic.

The first notes floated into the hushed air, delicate and pure, gradually building into a symphony of emotion, precision, and passion. It seemed effortless, as if the music poured from some divine reservoir within him. Yet anyone who knew Perlman's story understood the truth.

This breathtaking performance was not the product of natural talent alone but the culmination of years of disciplined practice, hours spent perfecting every phrase, every nuance, and every crescendo.

As he played, the storied violin, once owned by the great violinist Yehudi Menuhin before it became Perlman's, it seemed to resonate with more than just sound—it carried centuries of history, craftsmanship, and genius, blending seamlessly with Perlman's unparalleled skill and passion. The audience watched, spellbound, as Perlman delivered a performance that would become legendary—a reminder that true mastery is born not in ease but in effort.

Practice Slowly

For Perlman, mastery wasn't a single triumphant moment. It was the quiet, repetitive act of showing up day after day, even when it was hard, even when progress seemed invisible, even when his hands and body betrayed him. He kept practicing, refining, and returning to the music, trusting that each small effort, no matter how imperfect, would one day add up to something extraordinary.

Mastering the love language that matters most is no different. Like Perlman's violin, relationships require more than intention to create harmony. They demand effort, consistency, and yes—practice. To speak the love language and dialect your partner longs to hear isn't a one-time decision. It's an ongoing commitment. And let's be honest: you will miss a note now and then. Maybe routinely. You'll forget, get distracted, or let your own needs take center stage.

That's okay.

You'll need to give yourself grace and patience. Take it slowly. Itzhak Perlman once emphasized the importance of deliberate practice by saying, "One must always practice slowly. If you learn something slowly, you forget it slowly."

Learning to love well, like learning to master an instrument or a foreign language, takes time. It's not about rushing to get it right, but about embracing the process—one thoughtful step at a time. Slow, deliberate effort allows the lessons in love to sink deep, even when the steps feel small or imperfect.

What matters is that you return to the work. That you pick up the "violin" of your partner's love language—be it words of affirmation, quality time, acts of service, physical touch, or gifts—and practice. Again. And again.

The Imperfect Beauty of Practice

We leave you where we started: Mastering your partner's love language isn't about getting it perfect. It's about making progress. It's about making a consistent effort to show up, set your own agenda aside for the moment, empathize, and choose to love the person in front of you in the way they need most.

When you make a mistake, apologize if you need to. When you fall short, try again the next day. Each small act of love, practiced over time, fills your partner's love tank. It's not the soaring crescendos that matter most but the daily notes you play—the ones that remind your partner they are seen, known, and cherished.

To become a virtuoso of love is to embrace the imperfect beauty of practice. The missteps and wrong notes are part of the process, just as much as the moments of connection and joy. The true measure of mastery is not in perfection but in persistence.

And in the end, isn't that the real music of love?

About the Authors

Dr. Gary Chapman is the author of *The 5 Love Languages*, which has sold more than 20 million copies worldwide and revolutionized relationships across generations. A trusted counselor, pastor, and speaker, Dr. Chapman has spent his life helping people communicate love more effectively and build lasting connections. He is the director of Marriage and Family Life Consultants, Inc., and he travels the world presenting seminars. His radio programs are on more than 400 stations. He lives in North Carolina with his wife, Karolyn. Learn more at 5LoveLanguages.com.

Drs. Les & Leslie Parrott are #1 *New York Times* bestselling authors and psychologists. Their books include *The Good Fight, Your Time-Starved Marriage, Healthy Me, Healthy Us,* and the award-winning *Saving Your Marriage Before It Starts*. Their pioneering assessments have been used by millions worldwide and include the free MyHeartChart.com. The Parrotts' work has been featured in *The New York Times, USA Today*, and on *CNN, Good Morning America, TODAY, The View,* and *Oprah*. They live in Seattle. Learn more at LesAndLeslie.com.

Share the Love

Becoming a Five Love Languages Coach

If this book has stirred something in you—if you've found yourself thinking, *"I wish everyone could experience what I've learned here"*—you may be in a prime place to become a **Certified Five Love Languages Coach**.

This empowers you to turn your understanding of the five love languages into a practical approach and structure for helping others experience deeper connection and joy in their relationships.

For more than three decades, the five love languages framework has transformed countless marriages, families, friendships, and workplaces around the world. Now, you can be part of that movement—not just as a learner, but as a guide. Certified coaches are equipped to help individuals and couples discover their primary love language's unique dialects, recognize barriers to emotional connection, and apply simple, proven tools that bring real change—and with the help of a specialized coaching version of the 5 Love Languages Premium Assessment.

The certification process is straightforward and surprisingly quick. Through a series of engaging online training modules, you'll learn how to confidently walk others through the five love languages, ask the right questions, and offer personalized guidance. In just a few hours, you'll be ready to begin coaching with clarity and compassion—whether in a formal coaching practice, as part of your church or counseling ministry, or simply in your everyday circles of influence.

This isn't a program for everyone—and that's perfectly fine. But if you're someone who naturally listens, encourages, and wants to see others flourish, coaching may be your calling. Some coaches use their training to complement their professional counseling or pastoral work. Others serve couples preparing for marriage, families in transition, or individuals simply wanting to communicate love more effectively. The common thread is a shared belief that love, when spoken in the right language, changes everything.

And for many, it also opens a meaningful professional opportunity. Certified coaches often find that helping others through the five love languages can become a rewarding source of supplemental income. Whether you choose to integrate coaching into your existing work or begin seeing clients independently, it's a flexible and fulfilling way to earn while making a difference. You decide how much time to invest—some coaches meet with a handful of clients each month, while others build thriving part-time practices that fit seamlessly into their lives.

As a certified coach, you'll join a growing network of professionals, pastors, and everyday encouragers who are passionate about restoring relationships. You'll have access to exclusive resources, ongoing training opportunities, and the collective wisdom of a global community. Most importantly, you'll gain the joy of watching people light up when they finally *get* it—when love starts to connect instead of miss.

You don't need a background in psychology or ministry to begin. You just need a heart for people and a willingness to learn. The certification gives you the framework. Your empathy gives it power.

If that resonates with you—if you can imagine yourself helping couples or families discover new ways to love each other well—then perhaps this is your moment. Visit coaching.5lovelanguages.com to learn more, explore training options, and take your first step toward becoming a certified Five Love Languages Coach.

Because the love language that matters most might not only change your relationships—it could also become your way of changing the world.

Notes

1. P. D. Hibbert et al., "Are Root Cause Analyses Recommendations Effective and Sustainable? An Observational Study," *International Journal for Quality in Health Care* 30, no. 2 (2018): 124–31, https://doi.org/10.1093/intqhc/mzx186.
2. Paul Ekman and Wallace V. Friesen, "Nonverbal Leakage and Clues to Deception," *Psychiatry* 32, no. 1 (1969): 88–106. Also, Paul Ekman, *Telling Lies: Clues to Deceit in the Marketplace, Politics, and Marriage* (W.W. Norton, 1985).
3. This sentiment encapsulates his philosophy on life and communication. He shared this insight during a conversation with Benjamin Wagner, an MTV producer, emphasizing the importance of meaningful simplicity over superficial complexity.
4. John M. Darley and C. Daniel Batson, "'From Jerusalem to Jericho': A Study of Situational and Dispositional Variables in Helping Behavior," *Journal of Personality and Social Psychology* 27, no. 1 (1973): 100–108.
5. Richard Rohr, *Breathing Under Water: Spirituality and the Twelve Steps* (St. Anthony Messenger Press, 2011), xxiii.
6. D. A. Kenny and L. K. Acitelli, "Accuracy and Bias in the Perception of the Partner in a Close Relationship," *Journal of Personality and Social Psychology* 80, no. 3 (2001): 439–48.
7. Gary Chapman, *The 5 Love Languages: The Secret to Love That Lasts* (Northfield, 2024), 73.
8. Henry David Thoreau, *Life Without Principle* (Arthur C. Fifield, 1905), 5.
9. Walt Whitman, *Leaves of Grass* (David Bogue, 1881), 60.
10. "empathy," Dictionary.com, https://www.dictionary.com/browse/empathy.
11. J. Kruger and D. Dunning, "Unskilled and Unaware of It: How Difficulties in Recognizing One's Own Incompetence Lead to Inflated Self-Assessments," *Journal of Personality and Social Psychology* 77, no. 6 (1999): 1121–34.

12. Widely attributed to Ralph Waldo Emerson but original source unknown.

13. Widely attributed to Mother Teresa but original source unknown.

14. "E. B. White: Notes and Comment by Author," interview with Israel Shenker, July 11, 1969, *New York Times*; quoted in Scott Elledge, *E. B. White: A Biography* (W. W. Norton, 1986), 300.

15. Widely attributed to Christian Dior but original source unknown.

16. *Richard Evans' Quote Book* by Richard L. Evans ("Selected from the 'Spoken Word' and 'Thought for the Day' and from many inspiring thought-provoking sources from many centuries"), Quote Page 244, Column 2, Publishers Press, 1971).

17. Shelley E. Taylor et al., "Biobehavioral Responses to Stress in Females: Tend-and-Befriend, Not Fight-or-Flight," *Psychological Review* 107, no. 3 (2000): 411–29.

18. Helen E. Fisher, *Anatomy of Love: The Natural History of Monogamy, Adultery, and Divorce* (Random House, 1992), 28.

A perennial *New York Times* bestseller for over a decade—now with companion workbook!

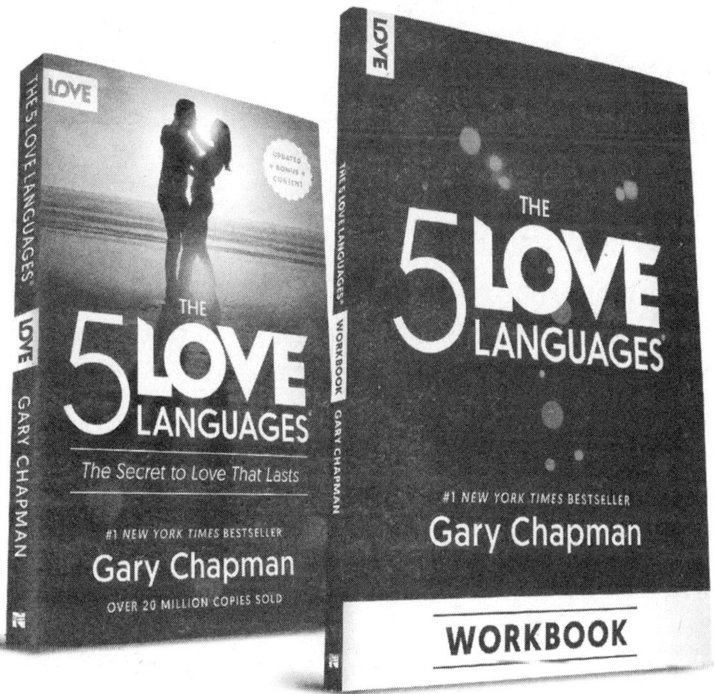

Combine the insights of *The 5 Love Languages*® with this practical, interactive workbook for deeper levels of joy and intimacy! With these two books, you will discover the secret that has transformed millions of relationships worldwide.

Also available as eBooks